# AWESOME UKRAINE

## Interesting things you need to know

7th edition

Kyiv
Osnovy Publishing
2019

УДК    908(477)(03)=111
Ц60

Authors of Awesome Ukraine Series — Hanna Kopylova, Dana Pavlychko
Executive editor — Nadia Chervinska
Authors of texts — Igor Makhtiienko, Victoria Linchevskaya
English editor — Daisy Gibbons
Cover illustration — Zukentiy Gorobiyov
Design and layout — Dmytro Ermolov, Dmytro Denyschyk
Photo editor — Anna Lysiuk

Osnovy Publishing
ilovebooks@osnovypublishing.com
www.osnovypublishing.com

Printing — Publish Pro, www.publishpro.com.ua

ISBN 978-966-500-843-9

# Foreword

With this book, we are pleased to bring you the sixth edition of
Awesome Ukraine. This isn't a typical travel guide — it's a celebration
of Ukraine's dynamism with pages devoted to major historical events,
sports, literature, cultural traditions, the beloved national cuisine,
and outstanding representations of Ukrainian art.

　　This book is being released during a time of war in the east of
the country and the illegal Russian occupation of Crimea. These,
unfortunately, are facts we must acknowledge. Ukraine's struggle
for independence continues as it tries to untangle itself from poor
governance, widespread corruption, and Russian colonialism. These
are hard times, but they are also uplifting times. Ukrainian art and
culture flourishes, its civil society is vibrant, its media landscape is
rich, and the food is really good!

　　Through this book we hope to give you insight into the country
we adore — one that is diverse, multi-ethnic, multicultural and
ever-evolving.

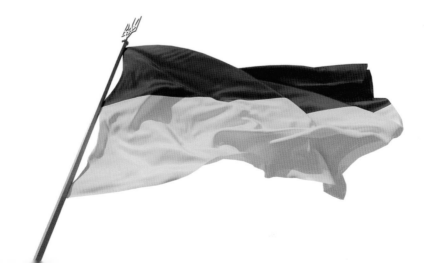

# CONTENTS

## HISTORY

## CULTURE

## FOOD

# HISTORY

*Right page: Unknown artist, **Kozak-Banduryst**, nineteenth century, the National Art Museum of Ukraine, Kyiv*

# 1

# The Blue and Yellow Flag

Ukraine's national flag was adopted on January 28, 1992

The flag consists of two equal-sized, horizontal blue and yellow stripes. It's a simple flag, but it conveys a powerful image — a shining blue sky over a fertile grain field.

While Ukraine's flag was adopted upon independence, its roots go further back. The blue-yellow color combination has been long used in ritual church decorations and as emblems of Slavic lands, princes, and noblemen. The thirteenth-century Halychyna-Volyn Principality emblem — a gold lion on a blue background — was based on these colors. Throughout the 1700s, the blue and yellow flag was used by Zaporizhian Cossacks, which raised its prominence.

During 1917–1920, the blue-and-yellow flag became the national flag of the Ukrainian People's Republic and of the Ukrainian state. Its adoption was brief. The Bolsheviks' victory in Ukraine brought a new flag — a red cloth with gold adornment. Despite this, the blue-yellow bicolor lived on as a symbol of the national liberation movement.

After the collapse of the USSR, independent Ukraine returned to the blue-yellow bicolor flag, a fact that is celebrated every year on August 23 with National Flag Day.

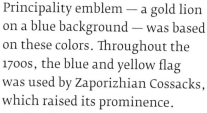

| | | |
|---|---|---|
| **PANTONE** | Process blue | 109 |
| **RGB** | 0.130.209 | 255.209.0 |
| **LAB** | 37.-33.-57 | 86.5.100 |
| **CMYK** | 100.10.0.10 | 0.10.100.0 |
| **WEB** | #0082D1 | #FFD100 |

# Tryzub

## Ukraine's national emblem

Like the majority of heraldic images, the *tryzub*, or *trident*, has a multifaceted and ancient history. The first drawings of the tryzub date back to the times of Trypillian culture (between 4800 to 3000 BC). The images can be found on pottery and symbolize a three-fingered deity. This is but one of over forty interpretations of the tryzub's meaning, ranging from the religious symbolism of the Holy Trinity to a stylized falcon.

In its contemporary form, the tryzub can be found preserved on the gold and silver coins of Kyiv Rus Prince Volodymyr the Great (c. 958–1015). Many of his descendants also used this heraldic image in their emblems and signs.

The tryzub repeatedly appears throughout Ukrainian history. However, it only became a national emblem in 1918 when it was adopted by the short-lived Ukrainian People's Republic (1917–1921).

In 1992, newly independent Ukraine returned to its origins and the tryzub was officially declared the state coat of arms of Ukraine.

You can get a tryzub hoodie from hip Ukrainian designer **Ksenia Schnaider**

# Vyshyvanka

## Ukrainians' fondness for embroidered clothing dates all the way back to pre-Christian times

These gorgeous embroidered shirts have long been treated as sacred and are passed down from one generation to the next. The vyshyvanka are believed to act as protective charms. Each individual shirt embodies centuries of Ukrainian folk culture with its unique symbolism and traces of ancient pagan imagery.

Traditional shirts come in various forms, materials, and types, according to their region of origin. The embroidery includes familial patterns and folkloric symbols that have a supposed prophetic quality, in that they are said to be determined by the future owner of the shirt and can tell their life story.

Vyshyvankas are seeing a popular resurgence. Ukrainian youth and contemporary designers have put a creative spin on traditional designs. While vyshyvankas are often worn on special occasions, you'll increasingly see them worn day to day as well.

Vyshyvankas can be purchased in traditional arts and crafts stores across Ukrainian cities and at fairs and markets.

*Left page:* **Jamala**, *Ukrainian singer,*
*winner of the Eurovision Song Contest 2016*

# 4

# ₴

# Hryvnia

## Ukraine's national currency is relatively new — it was adopted in September 1996

The hryvnia is a new currency, but it has ancient roots. It's thought that the word is derived from the Old Slavic *hryvna* — a piece of jewelry in the form of a hoop worn around the neck. Such hryvnas were commonly used by Scythians and early Slavs. The hryvnia's weight and form have changed across the ages. During Kyivan Rus, a silver bar weighing about 150 grams was called a hryvnia, and later on, from the eleventh to thirteenth centuries, the word was used to refer to the main currency — a hexagonal bar of silver.

The hryvnia was released into circulation in 1918, under the Ukrainian People's Republic. It was used until 1922 when Ukrainian lands fell under Bolshevik control.

Upon independence, Ukraine adopted a temporary currency — the kupon-karbovanets — which was subject to major inflationary shock. In 1996 Ukraine transitioned to the hryvnia.

One hryvnia equals 100 kopiykas. There are 1, 2, 5, 10, 20, 50, 100, 200 and 500 hryvnia banknotes in circulation, as well as 1, 2, 5, 10, 25, 50 kopiyka and 1 hryvnia coins.

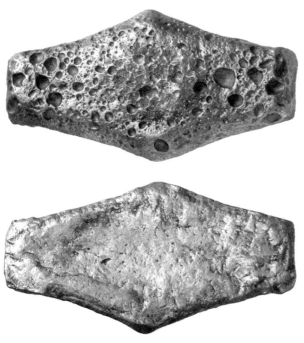

In 2011 Swiss financiers recognized hryvnias as *the most beautiful paper money*

Top: **Kyiv Rus hryvnia bar**, *twelfth to thirteenth century AD*
Bottom: **Two hryvnia banknote** *featuring Prince Yaroslav the Wise*

# Scythians

Nomadic people who lived in Eastern Europe and parts of Central Asia from the eighth century BCE to the second century CE

Two of the largest tribal confederations of Scythians were the Sarmatians in western Scythia and Amyrgians in eastern Scythia.

There is much debate concerning the origins of Scythians. Some researchers consider them an indigenous population, claiming roots in the Pontic-Caspian steppe. Others consider them to be migrants from Inner Asia. Either way, Ukraine is dotted with archaeological artifacts from the Scythian period. Scythian burial mounds, known as kurhans, are visible today in Ukraine and parts of Russia. These *kurhans* were built as repositories for powerful Scythian chieftains and kings.

Archaeological evidence reveals that *Scythians were fond of marijuana* — a tradition that they had imported from Central Asia

The Scythian and Sarmatian tribes may have given rise to Greek stories of *Amazons*. Kurhans with armed females have been found in southern Ukraine and Russia. Historians claim that many burials in the Don and lower Volga contained females dressed for battle as if they were men — a style that may have inspired the Greek tales about the Amazons

The Scythians were renowned for their ability to shoot their arrows with deadly accuracy from horseback. Scythian men would sport full beards and wear tall pointed caps, tunics, long coats, and pants tucked into their boots. Scythians are renowned for their fantastic gold work. They fastened it onto their garments in the form of plates; made it into belts, broaches, necklaces, helmets, earrings; and used it to embellish their weapons.

In 1948, an archaeological dig found that *Scythians wore extraordinary tattoos* depicting animals and scenes of nature

# Gold Pectoral

This remarkable example of early craftsmanship offers a glimpse into ancient Scythian culture

The Scythian Pectoral (meaning "necklace") came out of one of Ukraine's most famous archaeological finds. The Pectoral was unearthed from the Tovsta Mohyla burial mound in Dnipropetrovsk Oblast during archaeologist Borys Mozolevskyi's 1971 expedition. It was an incredible find. The burial mound, where Scythian elite were buried, held over six hundred pieces of gold jewelry and numerous other archaeological artefacts.

The Pectoral tells a story through its three bands with zoomorphic, mythological, and floral motifs. It also depicts Scythian men in typical garb — sporting beards, trousers, and boots. It's a must-see!

The Gold Pectoral is displayed in the Museum of Historical Treasures of Ukraine: 21 *Lavrska Street, Kyiv Pechersk Lavra* (situated right behind the Dormition Cathedral)

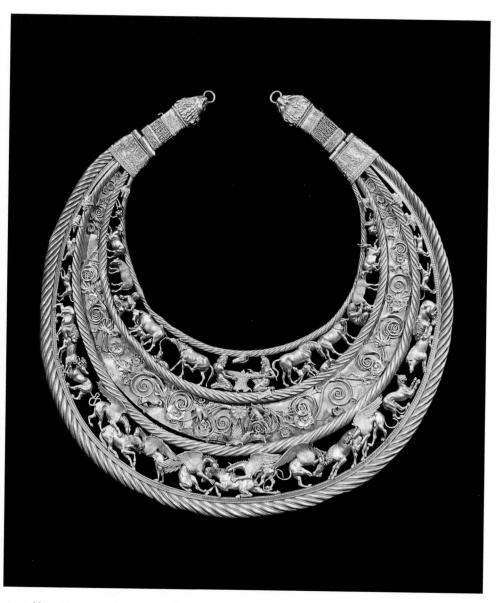

Top: **Gold Scythian Pectoral**, *the second half of the fourth century BC*
Left page: **Golden Hairpiece**, *from a royal kurhan in Solohka, next to Nikopol, fourth century BC*

# Kozaky

The Turkic word "kozak" (cossack) can be translated as "free man," "adventurist," or "highwayman"

Kozaks were also a military formation active in the fifteenth through eighteenth centuries both within Ukrainian territories and far beyond their boundaries. The kozaks' origins are disputed. The most popular tales place them as runaways, escaping from the oppression of their landlords. Warriors, peasants, and impoverished townsmen fled to the uninhabited steppes in the south of Ukraine where they took to cultivating land and herding cattle. They had to protect themselves and their property from the raids of the nearby steppe Tatars. In doing so, they honed their fighting skills.

By the beginning of the sixteenth century, the numbers of such seeking a better fortune increased. Cossacks evolved from being little more than

Top: Ilya Repin, **Reply of the Zaporizhian Cossacks to Sultan Mehmed IV of the Ottoman Empire**,
1880–1901, The State Russian Museum, Saint Petersburg
Left page: Still frame from the Ukrainian cult cartoon Kozaky (Ukranimafilm, 1967)

roving bandits into a noble warrior caste, a separate stratum of Ukrainian society, establishing their own center, the "Zaporizhian Sich," with its own laws and relative sovereignty.

Kozak imagery has been romanticized in art. In reality, they did not only protect Ukrainian lands from Tatar and Polish groups, but also led their own political games, fought each other, and through strong discipline and self-organiza-tion, acted as warrior mercenaries for hire by other countries. Russian Empress Catherine II used all the powers of guile in her struggle with the Zaporizhian Sich. On August 3, 1775, she signed a manifesto for its disbandment. One could be severely punished for even uttering "Zapor-izhian" or "kozak." Nevertheless, even now, brave, free-willed people, daredevils, and Ukraine's real patri-ots are called kozaky.

# Oseledets Hairstyle

## This fierce hairstyle is imbued with historical and cultural meaning

The *oseledets* or, as it is also called, *chupryna* or *chub*, is an ancient Ukrainian hairstyle. Men would shave their heads, leaving all but a lock of hair in the very middle. This hairstyle indicated the courage of its owner and his preparedness for war.

The first person to adopt this long *oseledets* — a word that actually means "herring" in English — is considered to be the glorious Viking Kyiv Prince Sviatoslav the Brave (935–972). In the time of Kyiv Rus this hairstyle indicated noble origin. But the general tendency to wear a *chub* entered its full popularity among Zaporizhian kozaks.

Kozaks didn't trim their mustaches. They greased and twisted them upward. With this look they demonstrated special *kozak honor and readiness to fight*

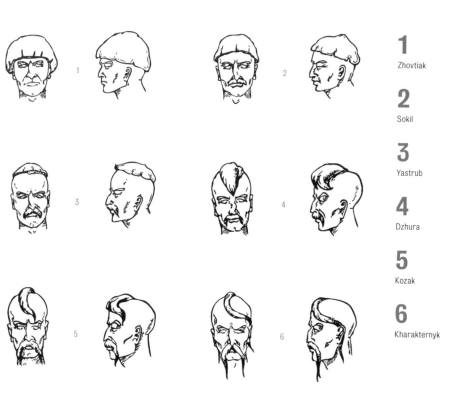

**1**
Zhovtiak

**2**
Sokil

**3**
Yastrub

**4**
Dzhura

**5**
Kozak

**6**
Kharakternyk

Sometimes the oseledets could reach to the shoulders, and it would then be wrapped around the head or left ear. According to kozak regulations, the chupryna was to be worn only on the left, along with one's saber. Depriving a kozak of his chub was considered a shameful affront.

In the Ukrainian artistic tradition, most kozaks, kozak leaders and hetmans are portrayed with bald heads and osedelets hairstyles. Like many past traditions, this punk-rock hairstyle is making a bit of a comeback thanks to the revival of kozak fashion following the Euromaidan Revolution.

One folk song states that a kozak wears a chupryna so that upon his death an *angel will carry him to Heaven by the hair*

9

# Sharovary

## One of the most striking elements of Ukraine's national costume

There is considerable archaeological and historical evidence that shows ancient Slavs wore such trousers as early as the tenth century. It is most likely that this fashion was borrowed and adapted from the Scythians or Sarmatians. The peak of their popularity was reached during the Zaporizhian Sich era. Sharovary were a part of equestrian military costume. Their specific billowing cut was designed so that a rider could move and navigate with ease — in case of danger, a rider would be unrestricted lest he need to quickly mount or dismount from his horse. Over time, these incredibly comfortable pants, along with jacket (zhupan), a linen shirt (cherkeska) and boots became the traditional kozak costume.

Despite the versatility of this traditional Ukrainian male costume, it is the word *sharovary* that generated the burdensome concept of *sharovarshchyna* — the superficial, shallow interpretation of Ukrainian culture, history, language, etc.

Today sharovary are profiled in some contemporary Ukrainian fashion collections. They are also worn by those who practice the Ukrainian war dance, hopak — otherwise known as cossack dancing.

Contemporary versions of sharovary have gained popularity with *fashionistas and hipsters* across the globe

*Ilya Repin, **Zaporozhets**, the Vitebsk Art Museum, Belarus*

# Anna Yaroslavna

## Highly educated, multi-lingual and politically astute, Anna was the sixth Queen of France

Anna Yaroslavna (born c. 1024) was the daughter of Yaroslav the Wise, the grand prince of Kyiv. He is sometimes known as the "father-in-law of Europe" because of how he established blood relations by marrying his daughters to the most influential European monarchs of the time. Like her siblings, Anna Yaroslavna also bore this fate. She married the French King Henry I, becoming the sixth queen of France. The French nicknamed her Anne of Kyiv.

Anna was educated, cultured, and known for her diplomacy in the conduct of affairs of state. Because of this, she had a hand in governing and her mark can be found on official documents from the time.

Anna Yaroslavna left *graffiti* *on the wall* *of St. Sophia* *Cathedral in* *Kyiv* in the eleventh century. It is preserved to this day

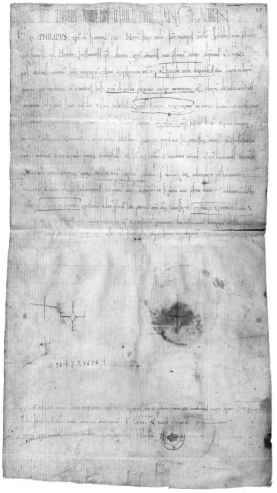

During Vladimir Putin's visit to France in May 2017, the president dated the French-Russian friendship back to the eleventh century, when Anna, whom the president called "Russian Ani," became the queen of France

Ukraine's official Twitter immidiately posted a response, pointing out that *Moscow didn't even exist at that time, so it doesn't make sense to call Anna Russian*

*A charter signed by Anna, 1063*

After the death of Henry I, Anna left the court for several years. She reappeared on the political horizon in France when her son Philip became king. Anna Yaroslavna's destiny after 1075 is unknown, yet this woman has forever entered the history of France not only as an impressive persona, but also as the great-grandmother of many French kings.

As the wife of Henry I, and as Regent for her son, Philip I, *Anna's signature in old Slavonic* can be found on official state documents from the period

# Chumaky

Hundreds of thousands of chumaky traveled along well-worn, north-south Ukrainian trade routes during the 16th–19th centuries

These traveling merchants would yoke two or four long-legged oxen onto a cart and set off to Crimea or to the shores of the Black Sea and the Sea of Azov in order to bring back salt and fish. About a ton of salt could be loaded onto one cart and then transported to cities and fairs across Ukraine. A *chumak* caravan (about a hundred carts) would leave in early spring and return in autumn. Chumaky were

*Top: Unknown artist,* **Chumaky**, *nineteenth century, the National Center of Folk Culture "Ivan Honchar Museum," Kyiv*
*Left page: The Milky Way, which is called the* **"Chumak Way"** *in Ukrainian*

often guarded by kozak troops due to the threat of Tatar raids in the southern steppes. In later periods, many kozaks would come to adopt chumak merchant activities themselves.

In the eighteenth century, chumaky monopolized the salt trade and made tidy profits for themselves. Several noble Ukrainian families started off as chumaky. After railroads appeared in Ukraine, there was little need for chumaky. They are now infrequently seen but often romanticized.

In Ukraine, the Milky Way galaxy is called Chumak Way. It bears this name thanks to a legend about chumaky becoming lost on their way home from Crimea. The astonished travelers witnessed some fallen salt fly into the sky, guiding them on their journey.

# Kozak Mamai

It's hard to imagine a more popularized image of the Ukrainian kozak than that of Kozak Mamai

According to legend, this kozak traveled the world and helps people. He embodied all the virtues attributed to the Ukrainian kozak: traveler, warrior, thinker, master storyteller, magician. Mamai was capable of curing wounds and lifting kozaks' spirits.

*A bronze monument to Kozak Mamai graces the Maidan Nezalezhnosti*

Kozak Mamai's portrait used to hang next to icons in almost every Ukrainian household. His visual portrayal is similar across thousands of paintings created by unknown artists throughout Ukraine. Mamai is always depicted sitting under an oak with a kobza (a type of lute) in his hands, a flagon and a cup resting next to him, a kozak harness hanging from the oak tree, and

*Unknown artist,* **Kozak-Banduryst**, *nineteenth century, the National Art Museum of Ukraine, Kyiv*

a horse feeding somewhere in the background. These images have been painted on canvases, on facades of houses, on window shutters, on furniture, and even on trees.

Hundreds of songs have been composed about this famous kozak, and he is celebrated in legends and fairy-tales. Some have even seen him as a saint. Many generations of Ukrainians have viewed him as their contemporary.

A great compilation of Kozak Mamai paintings can be found at the Ivan Honchar National Center of Folk Culture at 19 Lavrska street, Kyiv.

Mamai eventually came to personify Ukraine and *represented Ukrainians as a whole*

# Pylyp Orlyk

## Creator of Ukraine's first constitution, that established the democratic standard for the separation of powers

Pylyp Orlyk's (1672–1742) constitution was approved in the town of Bendery in 1710 and is known as the "constitution of exiles" because it was proclaimed by Ukrainian political emigrants. This constitution has served as the basis of many subsequent ones. It appeared sixty-six years before the US Declaration of Independence and seventy-nine years prior to the French Declaration of the Rights of Man.

Pylyp Orlyk was the right hand of Ukrainian hetman (leader) Ivan Mazepa (1639–1709) who, together with Charles XII of Sweden, fought against Russian tsar Peter I.

After defeat in the war against Russia in 1709, virtually the entire hetman elite emigrated to Bendery (an Ottoman-ruled town on the Dniester River). Upon Mazepa's death, the exiles elected Orlyk as their hetman. The newly proclaimed hetman — together with support from Swedes, Poles, and Tatars — attempted to free Ukrainian lands from Russian oppression. This attempt ultimately failed and Orlyk was doomed to the life of an emigrant.

While Orlyk's constitution never acquired legitimacy, the very fact of this document's cre-

The son of Pylyp Orlyk, Hryhir, became a prominent figure in France. He received the title of duke, was a member of the Royal Council of France and was Louis XV's confidant. The lands that formerly belonged to the Orlyks (fourteen km from Paris) are now the site of *the Orly International Airport* (Aeroport d'Orly)

*The last page of the original version of* **Pylyp Orlyk's Constitution**

ation marks a significant page in Ukrainian history.

In June 2011, on the fifteenth anniversary of the Ukrainian Constitution, a monument to Pylyp Orlyk was unveiled in Kyiv. A memorial plaque has been placed on the wall of his residence in Kristianstad (Sweden).

# Roksolana

From slave to the chief wife of the Ottoman Sultan, Roksolana managed to gain considerabl power and influence over affairs of state

Anastasia Lisovska (c. 1506–1558) was born in a small town in western Ukraine. As a young girl she was taken prisoner during one of the Crimean Tatars' raids and ended up at an Istanbul slave market. Later she found herself in the Sultan's harem where, by destiny or by fate, her womanly charms and beauty surpassed those of the hundreds of concubines in competition for the Sultan's heart and she became the wife of Suleyman the Magnificent of the Ottoman Empire (1494–1566).

This educated and capable native of Roksolania (Land of Ruses or East Slavs) ultimately acquired considerable influence over her powerful

Roksolana received the name **Hurrem**, *which means "the cheerful one"* in Persian

Top: *Still frames from* **Roksolana** *(Ukrainian Television Film Studio, 1997-2003)*
Left page: *Unknown author,* **Roksolana**, *ancient engraving*

husband and became a force in the Empire's politics. It was an unheard of "career" for a woman in the Muslim world at that time and astonished even European historical contemporaries. Roksolana is quite a controversial figure. According to historical sources and oral tales, in order for her son, Selim II, to inherit the throne, this "lady Macbeth" would stop at nothing — she sacrificed the lives of dozens of her husband's heirs and the lives of her own two sons.

# Bohdan Khmelnytskyi

## He shaped the future of Ukraine and the balance of power in Europe along with it

For many Ukrainians, Bohdan Khmelnytskyi (1595–1657) is one of the most powerful symbols of Ukrainian statehood and independence. To others, he's a traitor. Khmelnytskyi led the national war of liberation against the Polish-Lithuanian Commonwealth between 1648 and 1654. In 1649 he became hetman and the head of the Kozak state — remaining in this role until his death.

   In 1654 Khmelnytskyi signed a treaty with the Russian Tzar Alexei Mikhailovich to form a closer union between Ukraine

*A monument to Bohdan Khmelnitsky* is a dominating feature of Sophia Square. Built in 1888, it is one of the oldest sculptural monuments in Kyiv

Letter from Bohdan Khmelnytskyi to tsar Alexei Mikhailovich describes the victory over Polish troops and his desire for *a closer political bond with Moscovy*

Top: *Letter from Bohdan Khmelnytskyi to tsar Alexei Mikhailovich*
Left page: *Stepan Zemliukov,* **Portrait of Bohdan Khmelnytskyi**

and Muscovy. Eventually Ukraine was completely subsumed into the Tsardom of Moscovy and later into the Russian Empire. His diplomacy led to the gradual loss of Ukraine's independence to the Russian empire.

Despite this, amongst many Ukrainians Bohdan Khmelnytskyi remains the embodiment of a leader who could unite Ukraine against political, ideological, and cultural discord.

Khmelnytskyi had three wives, *two sons and four daughters*

# Crimean Karaites

## One of the smallest ethnic groups in the world

The appearance of Crimean Karaites in Eastern European territories (Crimea, Poland, and Lithuania) has been a subject of debate since the nineteenth century. Some argue that the Karaites are in fact Jews (both in the religious and ethnic sense of the term). Others claim that they are descendants of the Khazars, Polovets, and other Turkic peoples. According to one prominent theory, the Crimean Karaites, together with the Polovets and Kypchaks tribes, found themselves part of the Golden Horde where they from then on assimilated with the local population. In the thirteenth century, the Karaites came to Lithuania and western Ukraine (Halychyna and Volyn).

Today Karaites are one of the smallest ethnic groups in the world: there are about 2,000 Karaites of which 1,200 live in Ukraine. More than 600 Karaites live in Yevpatoria, Feodosia, and Saki.

The ancient Karaite cemetry in Chufut-Kale has existed for *1,500 years*. Currently there are 10,000 graves, making it
the biggest Turkic cemetery in Europe

One can find *a Karaite kenesa*
(a Karaite or Persian temple) built in 1902
at *Val Street in Kyiv*

In the sixteenth to eighteenth centuries there was an entire Karaite
principality in the medieval town of Chufut-Kale, situated in modern Bakhchysarai. There remains an ancient Karaite burial ground at the foot of this
mountain. It is considered one of the most beautiful cemeteries in Ukraine.

In nineteenth-century century Crimea, Karaites began to distinguish themselves from other Jewish groups, sending envoys to the tsar to plead for exemp-
tions from harsh anti-Jewish legislation. Later, they were considered non-Jews
by Nazis. This left the community untouched by the Holocaust, unlike other
Turkic-speaking Jews, like the Krymchak Jews, who were almost wiped out.

# The Ukrainian People's Republic

Ukrainian state founded in 1917 after the wane of the Russian Empire after the two revolutions in February and October of 1917

The Bolshevik Revolution in October 1917 suddenly radicalised the struggle for Ukrainian independence. When dual power was established in Russia, Ukrainian nationalist groups were able to come together. On March 4, 1917, a representative assembly for Ukraine, the Ukrainian Central Rada, was established under Mykhailo Hrushevskyi.

After the battle with the Bolsheviks, the Central Rada was able to retain power over Kyiv, and subsequently adopted the Fourth Universal on September 2, 1918, declaring the full independence of the Ukrainian People's Republic.

Although the history of the Republic was short-lived and rocked by state coups and the violent

*The Fourth Universal*, *adopted on the 2nd September 1918*

On August 22, 1992, Mykola Plaviuk, the president of the UPR in exile, handed a letter to president Leonid Kravchuk declaring the Ukrainian Independent State – which was proclaimed on August 24, 1991 – the successor of the UPR

In *the Treaty of Brest* on *February 9, 1918*, the Fourth Alliance recognized the independence of the Ukrainian People's Republic

events of the First World War, and the Republic was operating in exile for the majority of its existence after the Soviet Union took over the Ukrainian territories, it was incredibly important for the Ukrainian national idea.

The Republic was an attempt by Ukrainians to assert their right to independence, self-determination, and legislative autonomy, and to defend Ukraine's territorial integrity.

The foundations that were laid down by the Ukrainian People's Republic in 1917 to 1920 contributed to modern Ukraine's international legal status, which, when it was voted an independent state, became fully subject to international law.

# Nestor Makhno

Ukrainian peasant who became the father
of Ukrainian anarchism, and expert tactician
in guerilla warfare

From a young age Nestor Makhno, who was born in 1888 in Huliaipole
and died in 1934 in Paris, was interested in the ideas of anarchism. He
fought for the ideals of his Robin Hood-style "Union of Poor Peasants,"
for which he was arrested and imprisoned many times. During his incar-
ceration in the Butirskaya Prison in Moscow, Makhno read much political
literature and became acquainted with his fellow anarchist and future
adviser, Piotr Arshinov.

For the young Makhno there was only one aim: revolution. He believed
that the people could become sovereign of their own land without inter-
ference from politicians and political parties, and could instigate self-rule
through various professional and territorial *hromady* (local council, or soviet).
It was for this that he decided to fight.

In Paris Makhno ended up *working as a carpenter and light technician* for the stage of the Paris Grande Opera and for Pathé studio

*Nestor Makhno (right) and Pavel Dybenko, 1918*

In 1917 he returned to Ukraine and began his fight against the Ukrainian Central Rada as a counterrevolutionary entity. He created a rebel unit called the Black Guard and made three alliance treaties with the Bolsheviks in order to fight off the Germans, Austrians, Ukrainian Central Rada, Pavlo Skoropadskyi's Hetmanate, Tsarist White Guard, and socialist Directorate state. Although he had pretensions toward defeating the Bolsheviks, he remained independent from them.

The Makhnovites fought valiantly. However, history did not give the anarchists the upper hand, and they were forced to flee the country in 1921. Makhno was arrested in September 1923 in Poland, and was later freed. He spent his last years in Paris, maintaining his ties with the international anarchist movement, and was published in various anarchist periodicals.

# The Holodomor

Genocide of the Ukrainian people that was planned and upheld by the Soviet government, with the aim to smother Ukrainian national independence

Party expectations of grain yields in Ukraine were over eight million tons above the average harvest. Despite constant requests from collective farms to reduce government requisitions, no changes occurred, and party stipulations were to be carried out at all costs. Food stocks grew low and people started to starve. Ukrainian peasants naturally began to hide whatever they could, since party cadres would seize not only bread, but also potatoes, milk, and any food that was available in the countryside.

On August 7, 1932, the Law of Five Ears [of corn] was passed, whereby "theft" of collective farm property was punishable by death, which could be softened under "mitigating circumstances"

The fourth Sunday in November is recognized in Ukraine as *the Day of Remembrance of the Victims of the Holodomor*

*Top: Holodomor victims, Kharkiv region, 1933*
*Left page: Armed komsomol member guards a warehouse with seed stock, 1934*

to a sentence of no less than ten years; in essence, people were prevented from owning food of any sort.

The terror hit its peak in 1933, when starving peasants were prevented from leaving Soviet Ukraine or the Kuban region of Russia. According to the judgement of the recent trial on the Holodomor, the total human losses between 1932 and 1933 were 3,941,000 people.

Despite the Soviet policy of quashing discussion of the Holodomor, today the Verkhovna Rada of Ukraine, the UN General Assembly, the European Parliament, and a number of countries outside of the European Union acknowledge the Holodomor as an act of genocide against the Ukrainian people, created by the authorities under Stalin.

You can visit the National Museum "Holodomor Victims Memorial" at *3 Lavrska Street*

# 20

# The Second World War

Ukraine was made one of the founding states of the UN in recognition of the contribution made by Ukrainians in defeating Nazism

At the beginning of the Second World War, the territory of modern-day Ukraine was divided between five states: the USSR, Poland, Romania, Hungary, and Slovakia. Ukrainians in the Polish Army took action against the Wehrmacht from the first day of the war on September 1, 1939. In the secret Molotov-Ribbentrop Pact, the leaders of the USSR and the Third Reich divided between themselves the Polish lands, which included Galicia and Volhynia. However, Germany had different plans: on June 22, 1941, the German Army rolled into the USSR.

The Organisation of Ukrainian Nationalists (OUN), including those under occupation, made a considerable contribution to the struggle for Ukraine's independence during the war, but in the summer of 1941 OUN leaders were imprisoned in concentration camps.

The Ukrainian population lost more lives than Great Britain, Canada, the US, and France combined. It is comparable with *the current population of Austria*

The Ukrainian total loss of life is numbered between *eight and ten million*

*Khreschatyk Street during The Second World War*

In 1942, in Volhynia, Ukrainian nationalists created the Ukrainian Insurgent Army (UIA), which were guerrilla units that opposed Germany's plans for economic exploitation of Ukraine and the transportation of the population for forced labor abroad. Some regions temporarily freed themselves from the Nazis and were self-governing, under the protection of the rebels.

On September 21, 1943, Soviet forces reached the Dnipro River and were given orders by Stalin to take Kyiv, by whatever means necessary, by November 7, the anniversary of the Bolshevik Revolution. Kyiv was liberated on November 6, 1943, for which 380,000 soldiers paid with their lives. The battle for the Dnipro was the bloodiest operation in the war in Europe.

# 21

# Nikita Khrushchev

## Remembered for the expansion of the USSR's fledgling space program and a host of patchwork domestic reforms

Stalin's brutal regime had an absolute hold over the Soviet Union. After his death a power struggle ensued and Khrushchev became the leader of the Soviet Union — a title he held for a little over ten years. Prior to that he held several senior positions, including the position of first secretary of the Central Committee of the Communist Party of Ukraine (head of Ukraine in the USSR, 1947–1949).

Under Khrushchev's leadership, the political climate in the Soviet Union softened somewhat. Thousands of political prisoners returned home with gruesome tales of life in gulag labor camps. Khrushchev is remembered for his willingness to expose Stalin's repressive regime. He famously stated in what would be called his "Secret Speech" that "Stalin showed — in a whole series of cases — his intolerance, his brutality, and his abuse of power … he often chose the path of repression and physical annihilation, not only against actual enemies, but also against individuals who had not committed any crimes against the party or the Soviet Government."

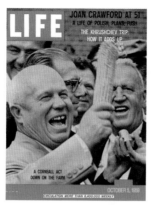

Khrushchev's famous idiom "*I will show you Kuzka's mother!*" at the UN assembly was translated literally. Its meaning was unclear, and since then the threat acquired a sinister nature. Subsequently the expression "Kuzka's mother" was used to refer to the USSR's nuclear bombs

*Khrushchevka* is a type of low-cost, cement-panelled or brick three- to five-storied apartment building which was developed in the USSR in the early 1960s

This period is sometimes referred to as the "Khrushchev thaw." But make no mistake, repressions continued. Freedom of thought was rather selective across the USSR.

Nikita Khrushchev is also known for presiding over the most intense period of the Cold War including the Cuban Missile Crisis.

Khrushchev ended up being pushed out of power and led a life of quiet retirement.

Khrushchev is particularly memorable to Ukrainians for his introduction of low-quality housing nicknamed "khrushchovkas" and for transferring the Crimean peninsula to the Ukrainian SSR in 1954.

# 22

# Independence Day

## Independence Day is celebrated on August 24 to commemorate Ukraine's 1991 Declaration of Independence

The Act of the Declaration of Independence of Ukraine was adopted by Ukrainian Parliament on August 24, 1991, establishing Ukraine as an independent state. On this day, Parliament called for an independence referendum to support the declaration. The resulting referendum on December 1, 1991 was unequivocal — more than 90 percent of Ukrainians voted in favor of independence with a high voter turnout of 82 percent.

Ukraine had sought independence from the Soviet Union for decades, and by the late 1980s, calls for democratic reform were overpowering. Several movements buoyed these aims. The Ukrainian miners' strikes between 1989 and 1990, and the Granite Revolution (also known

Today, Ukraine's independence takes on new meaning. Its centuries-long fight for independence continues with Russia's invasion of eastern Ukraine and its *annexation of Crimea*

**АКТ
ПРОГОЛОШЕННЯ
НЕЗАЛЕЖНОСТІ УКРАЇНИ**
*24 серпня 1991 р.*

Виходячи із смертельної небезпеки, яка нависла була над Україною в зв'язку з державним переворотом в СРСР 19 серпня 1991 року,
— продовжуючи тисячолітню традицію державотворення в Україні;
— виходячи з права на самовизначення, передбаченого Статутом ООН та іншими міжнародно-правовими документами;
— здійснюючи Декларацію про державний суверенітет України, Верховна Рада Української Радянської Соціалістичної Республіки урочисто проголошує незалежність України та створення самостійної української держави – України.
Територія України є неподільною і недоторканною.
Віднині на території України мають чинність виключно Конституція і закони України.
Цей акт набирає чинності з моменту його схвалення.

*Верховна Рада України*

*Top right:* **The Act of the Declaration of Independence of Ukraine,** *established Ukraine as an independent state*

as the Student Revolution) in 1990 supported the cause of independence.

Independence Day is Ukraine's most popular holiday, and Kyiv is a great place to take it all in. Put on a *vyshyvanka* (traditional embroidered shirt), drape yourself in blue and yellow, and head to Khreshchatyk for open-air concerts, parades, and other festivities!

Leonid Kravchuk served as independent *Ukraine's first president,* from December 5, 1991, until his resignation on July 19, 1994

# 23

# Orange Revolution

A series of protests and political unrest that took place in Ukraine from late November 2004 to January 2005

Ukraine's 2004 presidential election was marred by massive corruption, voter intimidation, and electoral fraud. This sparked a massive peaceful protest movement against the ostensible president Viktor Yanukovych and his party. Kyiv became the focal point of the movement's campaign of civil resistance, with thousands of protesters demonstrating daily.

Nationwide, the democratic revolution was supported by a series of acts of civil disobedience, sit-ins, and general strikes. It was organized by the failed presidential candidate Viktor Yuschenko and his party and supporters. The color orange was adopted to unite all those who fought against the corrupt elections, along with the word "Tak!" ("Yes!"). The nationwide protests succeeded when the results of the original run-off were annulled, and a revote was ordered, resulting in Yushchenko's victory.

*"Razom nas ba-hato! Nas ne podolaty!"* This chant spread through the crowd of hundreds of thousands that filled Kyiv's Independence Square during the Orange Revolution

*"Together, we are many! We cannot be defeated!"* emerged from a sea of orange, signaling the rise of a new demo-cratic Ukraine

*Viktor Yanu-kovych* holds the special status of sparking not just one, but two revolutions

The first, due to election fraud in 2004, and the second during the 2013–2014 Euromaidan Revo-lution when *he ordered protes-tors to be beaten and killed*

# 24

# Euromaidan

## Ukraine's Revolution of Dignity — a political, social and cultural transformation

Kyiv's Maidan Nezalezhnosti (Independence Square) is the city's central square — a meeting place to stroll, flirt, gawk and debate. It has long been the focal point for numerous protests and is, quite simply, the center of Ukraine's political consciousness. It was the site of mass protests against president Kuchma in 2001 and the Orange Revolution in 2004.

At the end of November 2013, president Yanukovych reneged on a promised trade agreement with the European Union, sparking a peaceful protest movement against this hasty reversal. A subsequent violent crackdown on peaceful protestors (along with the passing of draconian anti-protest legislation) cemented broadscale support for political change. The scope of the protests evolved over the coming weeks, and millions of Ukrainians came out on the streets to demand a democratic government. Widespread grievances of government corruption, abuse of power, violation of hu-

Euromaidan gave way to many cultural initiatives, among them *Artists Support Ukraine*, aimed at turning international attention toward the current situation in Ukraine

man rights, and profound economic mismanagement led
to calls for president Yanukovych's resignation. Through
the cold winter months, "Maidaners," as they came to be
called, set up camp, barricades, kitchens, medical services,
an open university, and even a library to support the cause.

Events came to a head at the end of January when several
protestors were killed. In the following month, more blood
was spilled — the regime's brutal Berkut (Eagle) special forces and government snipers killed dozens of men and women
and wounded thousands.

At the end of February, president Yanukovych gave an ul-
timatum to the protest movement — "pack up and leave
the Maidan." But the Maidaners remained, stalwart: they
weren't going anywhere. The deadline to leave came and went.
Yanukovych fled to Russia, and a provisional government
was formed.

*Serhiy Nigoy-
an* was an Ar-
menian-Ukrain-
ian activist. He
was the first
protestor killed
by shooting
during the Hru-
shevskoho riots
in January

# 25

# Russian–Ukrainian War

This conflict has claimed 13,000 lives (and counting), as well as 1,3 million internally displaced persons

After the Revolution of Dignity and Euromaidan movement, Russia began to engage in aggressive and unlawful armed actions that undermined Ukraine's territorial integrity. The Russian armed aggression consisted of its annexation of the Crimean peninsula in 2014 as well as hostilities in the Donetsk and Luhansk regions, which still continue to this day.

On February 27, 2014, unidentified armed persons seized the Supreme Council and the government building of the Autonomous Republic of Crimea and raised Russian flags on top of them. Later that spring, on March 16, a sham referendum was held to determine Crimea's status, whereby the vast majority of the population apparently supported the annexation of Russia. Neither Ukraine, the EU, or the US have recognised this vote as legitimate.

From the middle of April 2014, Russian and pro-Russian fighters began the battle to take a series of cities in the Donetsk and Luhansk regions. A pseudo-referendum on

The Ukrainian defenders of Donetsk airport — one of the bloodiest operations in the Russian-Ukrainian war — have earned the nick name "cyborgs"

On July 17, 2014, the Boeing 777 passenger flight MH17 from Amsterdam to Kuala Lumpur was shot down by Russian missiles over the territory of Donbas, whereby *all 298 people on board died*

the independence of the so-called "DPR" and "LPR" — the self-proclaimed Donetsk and Luhansk People's Republics — was held on April 11. From April 14, 2014, until April 3, 2018, an anti-terrorist operation was carried out, aimed at countering the war in Eastern Ukraine. Subsequently, the conflict acquired the title "The Operation of the United Forces."

The events that are taking place in Eastern Ukraine are an armed conflict that is being supported by Russia, which is supplying local pro-Russian rebels with military equipment, weapons, and soldiers. Due to the illegal annexation of Crimea and Russian aggression on Ukrainian territory, the international community condemned Russia, and on April 28, 2014, introduced additional and extended sanctions that were already put on individuals and legal entities from Russia and Ukraine directly involved in military aggression against Ukraine; they also installed an economic blockade of Crimea.

# CULTURE

*Right page: Mykola Pymonenko, **Fortune-Telling at Christmastime**, 1888, the State Russian Museum, St. Petersburg*

# 26

# Ukrainian Icon

## With Byzantine roots, icons have long held religious and cultural significance in Ukraine

The Soviet period — and socialist atheism — significantly diminished the role of icons for a time. But today this tradition has been revived and these holy images, embellished with beautifully embroidered *rushnyky*, are a common feature in Ukrainian homes.

Ukrainian iconography has a rich history. Having borrowed the basic techniques and style from the Byzantines, Kyivan Rus (the forerunner of today's Ukraine) developed their original interpretation. Alipiy Pecherskyi (c. 1050–1114) is one of the most famous iconographers to come out of the Kyiv School. The only creation of this outstanding master to have been preserved until today is the Svensk-Pechersk *Icon of Mother of God* that is currently in Moscow.

Ukrainian iconography has gone through various stages: from the original style of Halychyna icon, to the influence of European Baroque, to a western naturalistic style replacing the Byzantine tradition, as well as other borrowed artistic tendencies and a return to the indigenous traditions of Rus-Ukraine. Many older rural icons depart significantly from traditional iconography, offering depictions of everyday village life.

*Left page:* **Icon of St. Nicholas and the Archangel Michael at the Crucifixion,** *late nineteenth century, Western Ukraine (Bukovyna), private collection*

Many Ukrainian icons are considered to be *miraculous.* Some of them have been said to give off the scent of myrrh

Tales of *the healing properties* of certain icons abound, helping us believe in inexplicable miracles in our cynical times

A collection of icons can be found at the Museum of Ukrainian Domestic Icons in Radomysl, at *15 Pletenetska Street*

# 27

# Ivana Kupala

A colorful celebration of summer solstice, purification, fertility, and mischief

Ivana Kupala originated in pagan times and has long been celebrated on the summer solstice. Nowadays, it is celebrated in Ukraine on the night of the sixth to the seventh of July. After the adoption of Christianity in Kyiv Rus, this folk holiday began to take on religious connotations: John the Baptist's birthday coincided with this day, and that's how, over time, it came to be known as Ivan's (John's) day.

Despite its religious transformation, the traditions of this day have kept many of their pagan roots. Ivana Kupala festivities start with the creation of its central figures: Kupala and Morena.

The latter symbolizes a winter deity and therefore must be destroyed in the triumph of light and summer warmth. Participants of the festivities usually gather near a river with girls in flower garlands singing songs. Young men are set with the mission of destroying Ivana Kupala. In the evening a large campfire is set up for everyone present to jump over — a symbolic ritual of cleansing through the element of fire. At the close of the festivities, the girls drown the figure of Morena in the river and let their garlands, decorated with burning candles, float away on the water.

There is
an ancient
Kupala belief
that the eve of
Ivana Kupala
is the only
time of the
year when
ferns bloom.
Prosperity,
luck, success,
and power
would be
bestowed on
whomever
finds *a fern
flower*

# 28

# Holy Night

A Christian holiday celebrated on the night before Christmas

From ancient times, this night's traditions have been enveloped in an atmosphere of ritual and magic. On the Holy Night, people used to seek out special divine signs in their surroundings in order to predict their futures and made prognoses for the next year by means of various tokens. The rituals surrounding the Holy Dinner were considered especially sacred. Traditionally, the rich and hearty dish of *kutia* would be served, made from wheat berries, poppy seeds, nuts, and honey. This would be served along with eleven Lenten dishes — borsch, fish, pyrohy with cabbage, beans, potatoes, and mushrooms...

When the first star appeared in the sky, the whole family would gather at the holiday table. Some special rituals accompanied this extraordinary meal. For example, the men always gave some food from their table to their cattle, for they believed that this day every creature

According to the Julian calendar, Ukraine's Christmas festivities start on *January 6, Christmas Eve*, and end on January 19, with Jordan or Epiphany

could communicate directly with God and that no creature should be treated poorly. After the Holy Dinner, little children would set out to visit their godparents and exchange gifts with them. A dollop of kutia would be flicked onto the ceiling — the more that sticks, the better one's luck.

This festive holiday is still widely celebrated, though modern Ukrainians have preserved only a small portion of these traditions.

# 29

# Pysanka

## A symbol of life and rebirth since pagan times

*Pysankarstvo* — the art of decorating eggs with traditional symbols by applying wax and dyes in layers — is an ancient art form. Archaeological evidence shows that pysankarstvo has been widespread in Ukraine since the times of Trypillian culture (between 5400–2700 BCE), if not earlier.

In pagan times, pysanky, or decorated eggs, were associated with the rites of spring — symbolising life and rebirth. In Christian times this symbolism shifted toward Christ's resurrection and religious imagery. The old custom of exchanging these ornamented eggs around Easter time has been preserved to this day.

There are a range of *pysanka* techniques and methods and over one hun-

Address of the
Pysanka Museum:
*43 Chorno-*
*vola Avenue,*
*Kolomyia,*
*Ivano-Frankivsk*
*Oblast*

Cities across
Ukraine hold *py-*
*sanka festivals*
around Easter
time

dred symbolic patterns. Every curl and spiral in these designs holds meaning.

To learn more about the wonderful world of *pysanky,* you should visit the very unusual (and the world's only) museum dedicated to them in the Ukrainian town of Kolomyia.

# 30

# Wooden Churches

## From simple churches to gothic masterpieces, wooden architecture abounds

Ukraine has an incredible heritage of authentic wooden churches, with over two thousand of them! Wood is a short-lived material, yet remarkably, the oldest wooden church in Ukraine — the Church of St. Nicholas in the village of Kolodne, Zakarpattia Oblast — dates back to 1470! Though wonderful churches, cathedrals, and synagogues made of wood are scattered throughout Ukraine, the bulk of these exceptional architectural landmarks can be found in the western regions. Besides the unique wooden gothic churches of

In 2013 UNESCO added sixteen wooden churches to its *List of World Heritage Sites*

*The Church of St. Michael*, *eighteenth century, Ushok village, Zakarpattia Oblast*

the Carpathian region, there are also curious kozak churches in the Podillia region.

If you want to see these landmarks, you should hurry: during the years of Ukraine's independence alone, several hundred of these unique temples have been lost. The structures have been consumed by fire, intentionally destroyed, lost due to interconfessional quarrels, or damaged thanks to amateur "improvements" using plastic and metal plates that cause decay. It's a great pity that so much of this architectural heritage has been lost.

Great examples of wooden architecture can be seen in the National Museum of Folk Architecture and Life of Ukraine in the village of Pyrohiv at *1 Pyrohivskyi shliakh Street*

# 31

# Tsymbaly

## The tsymbaly (hammer dulcimer) is one of the oldest string instruments in the world

Cave paintings dating from 3500 BCE depict this instrument, indicating its ancient origins.

The hammer dulcimer arrived in medieval Europe by way of the Middle East. A European fondness for this instrument grew slowly over time. J. Shunda, who worked as a music master at the Hungarian royal court, popularized the instrument by constructing the first concert dulcimer in 1874.

In Ukraine, different kinds of folk tsymbaly became popular in the seventeenth century. They are mentioned in written sources and old folk songs.

The tsymbaly is generally an ensemble instrument. Its lively, dynamic character is an important part of dance music at Ukrainian holidays and weddings. Wedding marches, polkas, hopaks, *hutsulkas* for singing and dancing, *kolomyikas* and plenty of other melodies are played on tsymbaly. Folk tsymbaly are manufactured in Hutsulshchyna.

Tsymbaly playing is
popular in Canada
among the ethnic
Ukrainian diaspora.
There are a number
of musical com-
petitions, and the
instrument defines
"Ukrainianess" in the
local music scene

An exhibit of old Ukrainian tsymbaly and a collection of other unique folk instruments can be found at the Museum of
Theater, Music and Cinematic Art at: *21 Lavrska Street, Kyiv* (on the territory of Kyiv-Pechersk Lavra)

# 32

# Bandura

Traditional Ukrainian folk music is grounded in the rich and unique sounds of the kobza and the bandura

Until recently, there was little agreement on the common and distinctive features of these two plucked string folk instruments. It's now generally recognized that the *kobza* was developed prior to the bandura, which due to its greater perfection, all but usurped the kobza's position as Ukrainian folk music's favorite instrument.

Kobza-bandura players have been depicted in art since the twelfth century. The kobza gained popularity and prominence during the height of Ukrainian Kozak culture. Itinerant kobza players would perform songs in various genres. As a cultural phenomenon, this involved much more than singing and strumming a tune. *Kobrzarstvo* as a phenomenon provided the inner voice of Ukraine's common people. *Kobzars* were poets and chroniclers. These unnamed singers of Ukrainian history and culture inspired national dignity and unity. Given this role, it is no wonder that — when in the 1930's a campaign against Ukrainian nationalism was launched — many kobzars were arrested and disappeared.

*100 hryvnia banknote* featuring the landscape of Cherkasy Oblast and a blind bandura player together with a young guide boy

The most common type of kobzars were *kobzar-improvisers*; they performed well-known pieces differently every time... a form of freestyle

In reference to this tradition, a collection of poems by Ukraine's most famous poet Taras Shevchenko are named *Kobzar*

# 33

# Trembita

Until recently, the trembita served as the "mobile phone" of the Ukrainian Carpathians

As a communication technology, this folk mouthpiece instrument is of cultural and practical value. A classic trembita is over three meters long. Its sound can reach across dozens of kilometers. Given this, it's not surprising that trembita calls became the main communications signal for mountaineers. The entire life of a Car-

A trembita are listed in the Guinness World Records as *the longest wind instrument*, with some measuring up to eight meters in length

A real trembita is supposed to be made of *hromovytsia* — a tree that has been hit by lightning

A trembita has no lateral openings and therefore gives *the pure natural harmonic series of the open pipe*

Unknown author, **Hutsuls,** 1900

pathian village could be voiced with this pipe: from one mountain to another, shepherds shared important news, warned about danger, informed of new births, sent out wedding invitations, and accompanied the departed on their final journey with sorrowful melodies.

In the modern world of high-speed technology, this authentic instrument isn't in great demand — only musicians and collectors tend to set their eyes on it.

# 34

# Ivan Fedorovych

Ivan Fedorovych 1510?-1583 is the founding
father of Ukrainian printing

He created many of the first
texts to be printed in Ukrainian,
as well as other Eastern Slavic
languages. Fedorovych (back then
his last name was pronounced
in Russian fashion — Fedorov)
began his craft in the Kremlin,
in Moscow's first printing house.
By some accounts, he was forced
to immigrate to Ukrainian lands
because of fierce book printing
competition from local manu-
script copiers.

Ivan Fedorovych issued the
first prints of *Psalter* (1570), *Apostle*
(1574), *Ostroh Bible* (1581), the East
Slavic *Primer* (1574), and many other texts. These texts were of huge

Acts and Epistles of the Apostles (the Apostle), completed in 1574, is the first Ukrainian printed publication that has an exact date

*Fedorovychych's autograph* from July 23, 1583

significance to Ukrainian and European history and culture.

You will often come across Fedorovych's name in Lviv where he lived and worked for many years. The Ukrainian Printing Institute and one of Lviv's cen- tral streets were named in his honor. Lviv's biggest secondhand book market is situated near the monument to Ivan Fedorovych (13 Pidvalna Street). Rare books in Ukrainian, Polish, and Russian can be found there.

# 35

SHE

# Taras Shevchenko

## Ukraine's poetic soul

From Taras Shevchenko's (1814–1861) remarkable works spring an ideal and a conviction that a better life is possible: one that is free from social and political oppression.

Taras came from very humble origins. He was a poor serf, bound to serve his landlord, Pavel Engelhardt. He was emancipated thanks to the combined efforts of several well-known representatives of the artistic intelligentsia. His release was purchased for 2,500 rubles — a considerable sum at the time. Shevchenko went on to become a well-known poet, writer, painter, and activist. He joined the underground political organization Brotherhood of the Saints Cyril and Methodius, which led to his arrest and long exile. His powerful use of language and art has inspired generations to fight for a more equal, open, and compassionate society.

In the twentieth century, Taras Shevchenko's image as victim of the tsarist regime was actively cultivated first in Soviet, then in Ukrainian ideology. His frequent depiction as

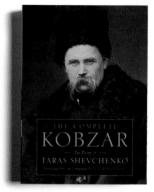

Kateryna is not only a painting. It is also one of *the most famous poetic works* of Taras Shevchchenko

Shevchenko's powerful poem *Testament* (*Zapovit*) has been translated into more than 150 languages

You can visit Taras Shevchenko National Museum in Kyiv at 12 *Taras Shevchenko Boulevard*

Left: **Kateryna**, 1842, the National Taras Shevchenko Museum, Kyiv
Right: English edition of Taras Shervhenko's **Kobzar**

a grim martyr conceals the real face of the genius artist — a Petersburg dandy and epicurean.

Taras Shevchenko's works profoundly influenced Ukraine's independence movement and continue to inspire nationalist-democratic ideals. Shevchenko's main work —

*The Kobzar* — is a "second Bible" for Ukraine's national movement.

Shevchenko's name adorns thousands of streets, squares, and even cities. His memory is honored by museums, prestigious awards, memorial boards, and over a thousand monuments worldwide.

# 36

# Lesya Ukrainka

A writer, poet, and feminist activist

Lesya Ukrainka (1871–1913), whose real name is Larysa Kosach-Kvit-ka, is one of Ukraine's most exceptional writers. She was a vastly influential writer, whose verses turned a new page in Ukrainian poetry and drama. Her works remain relevant to audiences today and are still regularly performed. Lesya Ukrainka was an avid activist in Ukraine's national movement. She advocated for Ukraine's independence from Russia — a theme that is prevalent in her artistic and published works. In 1902 she joined Ukrainian Marxist Organization and translated the Communist Manifesto into Ukrainian. In 1907 she was arrested and, following her release, was kept under observation by the tsarist police.

She was the second child of Ukrainian writer Olha Drahomano-va-Kosach, better known under her literary pseu-donym *Olena Pchilka*

On May 28, 2001, the National Bank of Ukraine released *a 200-hryvnia banknote* depicting Lesya Ukrainka

*Top: Lesya Ukrainka's family home in Novohrad-Volynskyi*

Folk songs and fairy tales provided the framework for *The Forest Song*, which is considered a highpoint of her artistic legacy It is still performed on theatrical stages in Ukraine and internationally.

There are six museums dedicated to Lesya Ukrainka in Ukraine, as well as numerous monuments that have been established in her honor, including those found in Georgia and Canada.

Her uncle, *Mykhailo Drahomanov*, was a famous Ukrainian political theorist, historian, philosopher, and public figure in Kyiv

# 37

# Ivan Franko

Founder of Ukraine's first political party, known by every Ukrainian as the "eternal revolutionary" of Ukrainian literature

Ivan Franko was not just a political figure, but also a writer, poet and translator – his creative output comprises of close to one hundred volumes, of which only fifty have been published. Franko was the founder of the Ruthenian-Ukrainian Radical Party, the first Ukrainian political party. He was imprisoned by the Austrian authorities four times for his political views and civic activism.

Franko had progressive views: he supported the Galician women's movement, and translated feminist works and supported the cultural and political emancipation of women. Although Franko came from the bourgeoisie, he preferred to spend time with the peasantry and because of this, he wasn't completely ac-

One of the regional centers in Western Ukraine, *Ivano-Frankivsk*, is named after Ivan Franko

Left: A monument to Ivan Franko in academic dress, Lviv
Right: Editions of Ivan Franko's books in different languages

cepted by both social groups — the former often finding his views too simple and the latter found him too intellectual.

Ivan Franko is featured on the Ukrainian *20-hryvnia banknote*

Even the way Franko dressed was a mix of traditional and innovative styles: he wore traditional embroidered peasant shirts — an essential part of Ukrainian national costume — with European three-piece suits.

Among Franko's most famous works is the play *Fallen Leaves*, the poem *Moses*, as well as the verse compilation *From Tops and Bottoms*. The majority of his works are included in the Ukrainian school curriculum, and Franko himself is seen as one of the greatest figures of Ukrainian literature. He was the first Ukrainian to be nominated for the Nobel Prize, in 1916.

# 38

# Johann Pinsel

He's called the Ukrainian Michelangelo, though why compare?

This incredible sculptor from Halychyna is a unique figure in the art world. Pinsel's life and creative path are enveloped in mysteries. It is known that he lived and worked in the eighteenth century in several cities of western Ukraine, but the years of his birth and death are unknown, and the very name of this sculptor is spelled differently across various archives.

Pinsel's sculptures tend to be carved out of wood and are created in the late Baroque tradition. They are considered masterpieces by art historians and are compared with the most outstanding works by European masters of this time. The dynamism and extreme expressions of Pinsel's sculptures — his subjects' faces tend to show great anguish and pain — are characteristic of his style.

In 2012 an exhibition of this outstanding sculptor's best works was presented in the Louvre.

In Ukraine, the biggest collection of Johann Heorh Pinsel works can be found in the Lviv Art Gallery and in the city of Buchach.

*Top: **Crucifixion**, 1760s, the Museum of Sacred Baroque Sculpture, Lviv*
*Left page: **Samson Tearing Apart the Lion's Jaws**, 1760s, the Museum of Sacred Baroque Sculpture, Lviv*

# 39

# Serge Lifar

This Ukrainian held a tireless devotion to his motherland, despite having lived abroad for most of his life

Serge Lifar (1905–1986) was born in Kyiv and at the age of eighteen, emigrated to Paris to work in Sergei Diaghilev's Ballets Russes. He was destined to become a real legend and a genius of twentieth-century ballet in France.

Lifar headed Paris's Grand Opera for more than three decades, staged more than two hundred performances, brought up a plethora of ballet stars, founded the Institute of Choreography in Paris, and occupied the honorable position of the president of UNESCO International Dance Council. Serge frequently wore a *vyshyvanka* to his premieres,

Lifar was *a ballet master of the Paris Opera* from 1930 to 1944 and from 1947 to 1958

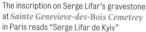
You'll find an exposition dedicated to Lifar in the National Museum of History of Ukraine at *2 Volodymyrska Street in Kyiv*

The inscription on Serge Lifar's gravestone at *Sainte Genevieve-des-Bois Cemetrey* in Paris reads "Serge Lifar de Kyiv"

called himself a kozak (his family had deep kozak roots), and repeatedly refused French citizenship that was offered to him by Charles de Gaulle. From the time of his emigration, Lifar long hoped to return to Ukraine — his wish was fulfilled only in 1961 when he had a chance to visit his motherland.

In 1994, the Serge Lifar International Ballet Competition was founded in Kyiv. As one of the world's most significant ballet forums, these competitions have launched the careers of many rising ballet stars and choreographers.

Lifar's memoirs, titled *Les Mémoires d'Icare*, were published posthumously in 1993

# 40

# Solomiya Krushelnytska

Wagnerian diva of the twentieth century
and the world's best opera singer

"The most beautiful and charming Madame Butterfly": this is just a sample of the abundant words of praise for Ukrainian singer Solomiya Krushelnytska. Born in 1872, she conquered the world with her luxurious soprano.

Solomiya was born into a family of a priest in western Ukraine and showed a propensity for singing from early childhood. When the time came for her to choose a profession, she entered the Lviv Conservatory and after graduation, continued her studies in Italy.

Starting in 1895, this Ukrainian singer performed triumphantly in top productions worldwide, across Europe, Africa, and South America. Her singing was admired by Fyodor Shalyapin and Enrico Caruso, Tito Ruffo and Giacomo Puccini. Solomiya Krushelnytska was the prima donna in many famous opera productions.

In 1920, at the peak of her fame, she left the big stage and traveled throughout western Ukraine to give chamber performances. When the Soviet authorities took over, Krushelnytska turned to teaching.

The Lviv Opera Theater is named after her, and a memorial museum has been opened in the apartment where she used to live.

In 1991 *an international competition* for opera singers was established in Lviv in her honor

*Giacomo Puccini* was a big fan of Solomiya Krushelnytska. Legend holds that her performance saved his 1904 Milan production of Madame Butterfly

Top: Lviv State Academic Opera and Ballet Theater of Solomiya Krushelnytska
Left page: Solomiya Krushelnytska on a Ukrainian postage stamp, 1997

# 41

# Shadows of Forgotten Ancestors

Love, tragedy and sorcery... all set to the rhythms of Carpathian village life

The 1964 film *Shadows of Forgotten Ancestors* was based on an eponymous novel by Mykhailo Kotsiubynskyi. Serhiy Paradzhanov (1924–1990), a Ukrainian-Armenian director, gathered a talented film crew and set out to the Carpathians. Their goal was to study and recreate the unique atmosphere and spellbinding spirit of Hutsulshchyna on screen. They spent time among authentic Hutsuls, absorbing their traditions and beliefs. Serhiy Paradzhanov, director of photography Yuriy Illienko, composer Myroslav Skoryk, performers of the leading parts Ivan Mykolaychuk and Larysa Kadochnikova, and the rest of the crew managed to create a truly unique film.

The film dreamily combines reality and fairy-tale. Rich in Hutsul folklore — with the sound of authentic Carpathian instruments and true-to-life characters (all the minor roles in the film were played by locals) — the film became one of the symbols not only of the Ukrainian poetic cinema period, but of the 1960s "thaw" and the new Ukrainian Renaissance.

The film has a powerful score. It features a variety of folk music using the most popular Carpathian instruments — *sopilka, floyara, kobza, drymba*. One instrument posed a particular challenge. In order to record the sound of the trembita, ten trembita-players with three-meter-long instruments flew to a studio in Kyiv. They could barely fit in the plane

In 2010, world-famous film director Emir Kusturica called *Shadows of Forgotten Ancestors* the best film ever made!

*Still frames from* **Shadows of Forgotten Ancestors**
*(Dovzhenko Film Studios, 1964)*

# 42

# Opishnia Ceramics

Cheerful and whimsical — Opishnia ceramics
are one of a kind

Pottery studios and schools proliferated across central Ukraine in the late nineteenth century. It was a popular craft in many towns and villages, with products exhibited and sold at numerous fairs. Amongst the various styles, pottery produced in the town of Opishnia in the Poltava region stands out. Opishnia ceramics were internationally renowned. In the beginning of the twentieth century a fifth of the town's population worked as potters, and during Soviet times it was home to a pottery factory.

The town is known for whimsical dishes in the shapes of different animals, particularly lions and rams. Opishnia was home to a ceramics school and many well-known ceramists such as Oleksandra Seliuchenko, Havrylo and Yavdokha Poshyvaylo, and Olha Shyian hail from this area.

Today, these traditions are kept alive. In early July Opishnia holds a pottery festival-fair "Zdvyh" with workshops, artistic competitions, and tours.

You can visit the
National Museum
of Ukrainian
Ceramics in
Opisania at *102
Partyzanska
Street*

Opishnia and
Kosiv (Ivano-
Frankivsk Oblast)
are the only
places in Ukraine
where *traditional
pottery is
preserved*

# 43

# Petrykivka Painting

A colorful celebration of beauty,
bounty, and nature

In the late nineteenth century an unusual form of decorative and ornamental painting flourished in Dnipropetrovsk Oblast. Its origins had a chaotic nature: to liven up their environments, peasants painted all their belongings, including their houses and ovens! Over time these traditions were transformed into a unique artistic phenomenon. Folk ornaments and folklore motifs traveled from walls to dishes, including porcelain and pottery.

In 1958 a factory dedicated to this art was opened — bringing these unique designs to a mass market. It produced artistic and household products for export to more than eighty countries. In its prime souvenirs with Petrykivka paintin became the thing to get if you wanted Ukrainian folk art.

The factory stopped production in the early twenty-first century, and in 2011 it was destroyed altogether and machines were removed. Despite this, more than two hundred residents of Petrykivka continue painting in this tradition, drawing inspiration from the works of such Petrykivka folk artists as Nadiia Bilokon, Fedir Panko, and Tetiana Pata.

Petrykivka painting is highly valued in parts of Asia, particularly in *China and Japan* where there have been very successful exhibitions of Petrykivka products

# 44

# Vladyslav Horodetskyi

A creative, whimsical, and imaginative architect, entrepreneur, and philanthropist

Vladyslav Horodetskyi (1863–1930) is of Polish descent, but he made Kyiv his home for thirty years and left an incredible architectural mark on the city. Horodetskyi designed buildings and entire streets. His most famous creations are the National Art Museum, the House with Chimaeras, and the St. Nicholas Roman Catholic Cathedral built in pseudo-gothic style. Many consider the House with Chimaeras the most unique building in Kyiv. This architectural and sculptural masterpiece is built on a steep slope, and its facade is ornamented with dozens of concrete animals and mythological creatures. Besides his work in Kyiv, Horodetskyi has also designed buildings in Cherkasy, Uman, and other Ukrainian cities.

Thanks to the renowned architect's devotion to Art Nouveau, he was nicknamed "Kyiv's Gaudi." One of the main streets in Kyiv is named in his honor.

After the arrival of Soviet authorities, the architect emigrated first to Poland and then to Teheran where he designed several remarkable buildings, including the Shah's palace.

House with
Chimaeras
*10 Bankova
Street, Kyiv*

# 45

# Witch

## Witches have always held a prominent role in Ukrainian mythology

The word *witch* derives from the Old Rus term "вѣдъ" — "to know." This points to the fact that in ancient times, witches were women who possessed sacred knowledge of the world. Later, attitudes toward witches shifted to take on negative connotations. While Ukraine never saw large-scale witch hunts of the type that occurred in Catholic and Protestant Europe, witches did, over time, fall into disfavor.

In the Ukrainian folk tradition, witches are divided into those who are "born" and those who are "taught." It was believed that former witches could be identified by inspecting them for signs of a tail. Both "taught" and "born" witches were thought to have

Viy: a young theology student is ordered to preside over the wake of *a witch in a small old wooden church* in a remote Ukrainian village

*Still frame from 1967 cult horror classic* **Viy** *(Mosfilm, 1967)*

a ranking order of powers, with the weakest witches capable of little more than stealing milk from cows, and more powerful ones able to mistreat people in various ways (e.g., induce disease and change the weather). The most qualified witches were thought to possess even greater skills. On the night of Ivana Kupala, legends tell that they would fly to Bald Mountain in Kyiv for the Witch's Sabbath. To this day, this mountain is a meeting point for fantasy fans, paganists, Satanists and Wiccans — keeping the spirit of magic alive.

# 46

# Leopold von Sacher-Masoch

The author whose name provided a title to a whole concept in psychiatry and sexopathology

When Lviv, Prague, and even Venice shared borders and were all ruled from Vienna by the Habsburg dynasty, people born in these cities became Austrians by default. The Austrian writer Leopold von Sacher-Masoch (born in Lemberg, modern-day Lviv), wasn't spared this fate, although, according to some sources, his mother was Ukrainian and his father had distant Spanish roots.

Sacher-Masoch's links to the area were short-lived, yet Halychyna (the region around Lviv, Ternopil, and Ivano-Frankivsk) was a central feature of his literary work. Many of his stories depict everyday life in Halychyna and the semantics of Eastern European sexuality. Many places in Lviv are associated with Sacher-Masoch's persona.

Tourists might be particularly interested in the thematic Masoch-Cafe, which is designed as a museum of eroticism and masochism — a monument to the author graces the entrance. Many of Lviv's theaters keep

Wanda von Sacher-Masoch, a long-time fan of Sacher-Masoch, *became his wife*

In the nineteenth century about *fifteen of Sacher-Masoch's works* were published in Halychyna

*Clockwise: Masoch-Cafe, 7 Serbska Street, Lviv; Wanda von Sacher-Masoch; Leopold von Sacher-Masoch*

Sacher-Masoch's memory alive by staging performances based on his works. The famous Grand Hotel in central Lviv replaced the building where von Sacher-Masoch was born.

# 47

# Les Kurbas

## One of the most important Ukrainian theater directors of the twentieth century and a member of the Executed Renaissance

Upon Ukraine's independence there was an explosion in the creative sector: new theaters were founded; extraordinary artists emerged; directors such as Roman Viktiuk and Andriy Zholdak found international recognition; and international festivals such as Golden Lion, Drabyna, Kyiv Travnevyi, and Gogolfest grew in popularity. Contemporary theater in Ukraine owes much to Les Kurbas (1887-1937), the father of Ukrainian theater, who is considered to be one of the lead figures of the Executed Renaissance.

Between 1917–1918, Molodyi Teatr (Young Theater) was founded in Kyiv. In 1922 it grew into the brainchild of theater director and actor Les Kurbas and was renamed Berezil (meaning "Spring" or "New Beginning"). As devotees of the avant-garde, this theater group gradually became the embodiment of experimental theater and, naturally, a target of Bolshevik repression. For ordinary audiences accustomed to simpler artistic forms, Kurbas and his theater's deeply philosophic productions seemed

Today you can visit Les Kurbas Academic Theater in Lviv. In Kyiv — *the National Center for Theater Arts* also carries his name, and the small stage of the Taras Shevchenko Academic Theater in Kharkiv is called the Berezil theater

Top: *The Berezil performance Narodnyi Malakhii*
Bottom: *The Berezil theater movement class*

foreign. Nevertheless, theater the Berezil theater was fortunate to stage a series of outstanding performances based on plays by European classics (W. Shakespeare, H. Ibsen, F. Shiller, Moliere) and on works by Ukrainian playwrights, particularly, Mykola Kulish — first in Kyiv, then in Kharkiv.

The avant-garde pursuits of these distinguished reformers of their time ended in tragedy. In autumn 1937, Les Kurbas, Mykola Kulish and thousands of prominent figures of Ukrainian culture, after spending years in the Solovki prison camp, were shot in Sandarmokh in Karelia in northern Russia. For this they are known as the Executed Renaissance — a whole generation of writers and artists wiped out by Stalin's regime.

# 48

# The Executed Renaissance

An entire generation of Ukrainian artists and prominent cultural figures of the 1920-30s who became victims of the Stalinist regime

During the interwar period, Ukraine was part of the USSR, and the Soviet authorities forced this new generation of writers and artists to comply with the demands of the totalitarian regime, suppressing their freedom of speech and any dissent. However, the new intellectual elite in Ukraine started to doubt the ideals of the revolution and tried to create a distinctive and indepen-dent identity according to their own creative and social values. The Soviet authorities, on the other hand, saw this as a threat and thus began to clamp down on Ukrainian artists.

The year 1933 is considered the beginning of the mass crackdown of the Ukrainian creative elite, when Mykhailo Yalovyi was arrested and Mykola Khvylovyi took his own life in the Kharkiv House of Writers, "Slovo." The repressions reached their height in 1937, when dozens of Ukraine's major cultural figures were shot after being denounced as "bourgeois Ukrainian

It was *Yezhy Gedroiiets* who came up with the term the Executed Renaissance for an anthology of Ukrainian litera-ture between 1917 and 1933

*Top: The members of VAPLITE, 1926*
*Left page: Kharkiv House of Writers "Slovo"*

nationalists." Among their number were Les Kurbas, Mykola Kulish, Valerian Pidmohylnyi, and Marko Voronyi. Avantgarde writers Mikhail Semenko, Yevhen Pluzhnyk, and Mykola Zerov were also subject to these repressions, as well as artists Mykhailo Boichuk, and Mykola Ivasiuk.

The authorities also forced many other Ukrainian cultural representatives to denounce their views and to endorse the regime in their work in order to survive. Others were able to emigrate, and fled the country.

Ukraine's best and brightest were wiped out by the Stalin regime, both physically and morally. The development of art, literature, and theater returned to primitive standards: there was to be no deviation from the norm of Socialist Realism, no sense of individuality. Instead, everyone had to conform to the collective Socialist ideal and the ruling establishment.

The members of *the literary union VAPLITE* (Free Academy of Proletarian Literature or Vilna Akademia Proletarskoi Literatury) became one of the first victims of the Stalin regime's repressions

# 49

# Oleksandr Dovzhenko

The Swedes have Bergman, Russians — Tarkovsky, the French — Godard, Italians — Fellini, and the English have Hitchcock...

Here, Ukraine is worthily represented by Oleksandr Dovzhenko (1894–1956). Despite the evident Soviet patriotic sentiment permeating films by this renowned director, the global artistic community received his first works with affection. His grandiose films *Zvenyhora* (1928) and *Earth* (1930) brought Dovzhenko real recognition. European filmmakers used to call him the "Homer of Cinema."

Other than achievements in directing, Dovzhenko is also known for his prose. In cooperation with his wife Yulia Solntseva, he made several feature films based on his own adaptations — bringing fame to Ukrainian cinema.

However, at the beginning of World War II Dovzhenko fell into Stalin's disfavor. Soviet censorship banned his films, cut his scripts, and made completing the projects he started impossible. He turned his pursuits to writing instead.

In the late 1950s Dovzhenko's film Earth was included in the list of *12 best films in world* filmmaking history

Dovzhenko's film Earth shocked viewers with *famous nude scenes* in the finale

*Top: Dovzhenko filming his ground breaking film **Earth** (Mosfilm, 1930)*
*Bottom: Still frames from **Earth** (Mosfilm, 1930)*

# 50

# Mariya Prymachenko

## A dream world of fairy tales, folk legends, and mythical beasts

Mariya Prymachenko (1909-1997) and her representations of folk primitivism have gained world-wide acclaim. Prymachenko was born into a peasant family. She grew up surrounded by artistically gifted people, and her interest in making art began quite early in life. Over time, she transformed as an artist and came to astonish the art scene that was gathered at the 1937 Paris art exhibition. Her talent enchanted Picasso, Chagall, and many others who greatly admired the extraordinary nature of her naive art.

Her works commonly represent a struggle between good and evil, life and death, happiness and sadness. Those with an eye for beauty will see an entire universe created by exceptional imagination, inhabited by whimsical birds, animals, plants, and fantastic creatures. She often anthropomorphised animals in her work, giving them inquisitive eyes and long eyelashes. Mariya Prymachenko's unique and compelling perspective transformed Ukraine's long tradition of folk imagery.

Mariya was born in 1909 and spent all her life in the village of Bolotnya, situated *30 km from Chornobyl*

In 1986 she created an impressive *Chornobyl series*

2009 was announced the *Year of Mariya Prymachenko* in Ukraine (by UNESCO)

Most of Mariya Prymachneko's paintings are followed with short poems depicting a colorful life of *people, animals, and plants*

Top: **Lazy Fellow Under an Apple Tree**, *1968*
Bottom: **Animal on a Stroll**, *1971*

# 51

# Oleksandr Arkhypenko

One of Ukraine's most outstanding artists whose expression was silenced during Soviet times

This sculptor's immense impact on the world of art was not just left unacknowledged by Soviet officials, but was also denied recognition in the official art history of the USSR.

A native of Kyiv, Oleksandr Arkhypenko (1887–1964) moved to Paris at a young age. He would later relocate to the United States and become a recognized master and founder of cubism in sculpture. He founded a school of plastics and taught at the Chicago School of Industrial

♀ Address of the National Art Museum in Kyiv — *6 Hrushevskoho Street*

Left: **Flat Torso**, 1914
Right: **Femme assise (Composition)**, 1920

Archipenko departed from the neo-classical sculpture of his time and created *a new way of looking at the human figure*, showing a number of views of the subject simultaneously

Arkhypenko is known for *mixing genres and experimenting with materials* such as clear acrylic and terracotta

The artist's collection, presented at the World's Fair Chicago, was estimated at *$25,000*

Arts and at the University of Kansas. Oleksandr Arkhypenko was a pioneer of "archipeinture"; he introduced negative space, polychromy, and synthetic moving constructions in sculpture.

Arkhypenko had more than 130 personal exhibitions in his lifetime. In Ukraine, his works are displayed in the National Art Museum of Ukraine in Kyiv and in the National Museum in Lviv.

Address of the National Museum in Lviv — *20 Svobody Avenue*

# 52

# Kazimir Malevich

An avant-garde artist and theoretician
of Ukrainian-Polish descent

Kazimir Malevich (1879–1935) the leader of the avant-garde suprematist movement. Malevich was born in Kyiv and spent his childhood moving around Ukraine with his family. At the age of sixteen, he began studying at the Mykola Murashko Kyiv Drawing School. In 1904, Malevich moved to Moscow and participated in several exhibitions. In 1915, Kazimir Malevich started a new trend in art: suprematism. His most iconic work in this style is the renowned *Black Square* painting.

From 1919 to 1930, Malevich taught and wrote. He taught at the Vitebsk Practical Art School in the USSR, which was headed

*Malevich's works are held in several major art museums, including the State Tretyakov Gallery in Moscow, and in the Museum of Modern Art and the Guggenheim Museum in New-York*

*Kazimir Malevich,* **Black Square,** *1915, the State Tretyakov Gallery, Moscow, Russia*

by Marc Chagall at the time. He was also one of the founders of the State Institute of Artistic Culture in Leningrad, and taught at the Kyiv Art Institute. Malevich passed away in Leningrad in 1935, leaving behind not only outstanding works of art, but also a considerable body of literature.

Suprematist Composition by Malevich was sold at a Sotheby's auction for more than *$60 million* in 2008

53

# Volodymyr Horovyts

It's hard to imagine a musical career
more successful than that of Kyiv native
Volodymyr Horovyts

Volodymyr Horovyts (1903–1989) began his career as a composer and later worked as a pianist in order to feed his family
during the difficult post-revolutionary years. Having emigrated to the West in 1925, Volodymyr Horovyts earned world
fame as a musician. There were times when he would give 350
concerts a year, performing classical music. Audiences would
break their chairs in astonishment during his concerts in Paris. After his performance at Carnegie Hall, twenty-five-year-old
Volodymyr Horovyts won the US over with his talent and virtu-
oso technique. In 1943, he raised a record-breaking sum of $11
million at a charity concert for the war effort.

Horovyts was widely successful and accomplished.
Since 1962, he has received twenty-four  Grammy Awards,
and in 1986, American president Ronald Reagan honored him
with the presidential Medal of Freedom.

In 1986, Horowitz
was awarded
*the Medal
of Freedom*
(the highest
award that can be
bestowed
upon a US
civilian).
In that same
year he returned
to the USSR
for the first time
in sixty-one years
for a series

# 54

# Mykola Pymonenko

## Probably the best representative of the Ukrainian school of genre painting

Mykola Pymonenko (1862–1912) began his creative path as a child by studying iconography. He was noticed by Ukrainian artist and mentor Mykola Murashko and was accepted to the Kyiv Drawing School free of charge. Within two years he was offered a prestigious tutor position at his alma mater.

Upon completing drawing school, Mykola Pymonenko continued his studies at the renowned Imperial Academy of Arts in St. Petersburg. In 1884 he returned to his homeland to teach at the School of Drawing school and work on his own art.

Mykola Pymonenko was a member of the Peredvizhniki (Wandering Artists) movement. Thanks to his vivid, realistic representations and exceptional knowledge of everyday urban and village life, his paintings were highly successful in Ukraine and internationally. His work has been exhibited in many international shows and is particularly praised in Russia.

Over seven hundred of Pymonenko's works adorn museums worldwide.

His work, *A Fabric Trading Woman*, was sold for $16,000 at an auction in the United States — a record-setting price for one of his works.

Clockwise: **A Fjord**, 1901, the Odesa Museum of Art
**Harvest Gathering in Ukraine**, 1896, the Volgograd Fine Arts Museum
**Fortune-Telling at Christmastime**, 1888, the State Russian Museum, St. Petersburg

# 55

# Volodymyr Ivasiuk

## A legendary Ukrainian poet and composer who befell a tragic fate

While his life was cut short — at only thirty years — his songs have left an enduring legacy. "Chervona Ruta," "I'll Go Far into the Mountains," "Vodohray" and his other works became real hits in their time and are widely recognized today. Endowed with many talents, Ivasiuk (1949–1979) became one of the founders of Ukrainian pop music. Renowned singer and National Artist of Ukraine Sofia Rotaru often performed his songs, widely popularizing them both before and after independence.

In May 1979, Ivasiuk's body was found hanged in the Bryukhovetskyi forest in Lviv. While the official line purported this to be a suicide, there is evidence to suggest that Ivasiuk was killed on KGB orders. The day of this famous poet

Volodymyr Ivasiuk
Memorial Museum
is situated at *40/1*
*Mayakovskogo*
*Street,*
*Chernivtsi*

*Volodymyr Ivasiuk together with Soviet and Ukrainian pop diva Sofia Rotaru*

and composer's funeral was marked by a mass protest against the Soviet regime. Following this mobilization, Ivasiuk's work was banned.

Nowadays Volodymyr Ivasiuk's memory is honored through numerous events, awards, monuments, posthumous titles, etc. But the greatest recognition of his contributions comes from his enduring legacy — generations of fans continue to love Ivasiuk's songs. They've stood the test of time.

# 56

# Mykola Syadrysty

Imagine a book that consists of twelve pages sewn together with a spider web, and a 0.6 millimeter book cover made of an immortelle flower petal

This microminiature version of Taras Shevchenko's *Kobzar* is the smallest book in the world. Its creator is the legendary Ukrainian guru of micro miniatures, Mykola Syadrysty (born in 1937).

It is thanks to M. Syadrysty's work that the very word "microminiature" now appears in encyclopedias and dictionaries. Syadrysty is considered the founder of this art, although microminiature actually existed before.

Syadrysty created the world's smallest chess set, a caravan of camels fitted into the eye of a needle, a rose inside a single drilled hair, the famous "shoed flea," and watercolor portraits of well-known people on the edges of pear and apple seeds. Every piece is created manually with Mykola Syadrysty's personally-invented technology and unique instruments. The author reveals the secrets of his masterpieces'

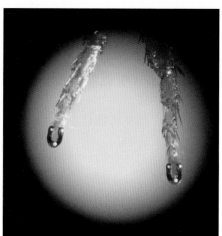

An exhibition of Mykola Syadrysty's works in Kyiv is situated on the territory of the Kyiv-Pechersk Lavra at *21 Mazepa Street.* Miniature exhibits are equipped with unique optic systems that allow visitors to have a good look at them

Widely considered the world's best microminiaturist, Mykola Syadrysty has a lifetime's worth of tiny creations on display in this museum: a tray complete with a wine bottle and glasses, all set on a grain of salt, or *a flea shod with golden horseshoes*

creation in his books: *Is It Difficult to Shoe a Flea? (1966)* and *Secrets of Microtechnique (1969).*

This unique art form is but one of Syadrysty's passions — for many years he has been researching the history of totalitarian regimes.

Permanent exhibitions of Mykola Syadrysty's works are open in Kyiv, at the Moscow Polytechnic Institute and in the Museum of Microminiature in Andorra.

# 57

# Bohdan Stupka

This acclaimed actor inspired an entire
era of Ukrainian theater and film

Bohdan Stupka (1941–2012) made his cinematic debut in 1971 in the cult Ukrainian film *White Bird with a Black Mark*. He went on to become one of the most prominent film actors of the Ukrainian SSR, and later, the face of independent Ukrainian film. He also starred in prominent foreign films under such directors as Otar Iosseliani, Krzysztof Zanussi, Régis Wargnier, Jerzy Hoffman, and others. During his career, Bohdan Stupka performed more than one hundred roles in film and as many works in theater.

From 1961, Stupka dedicated seventeen years to Maria Zankovetska's Lviv Academic Drama Theater. He would later go on to follow in the footsteps of his mentor, the famous Ukrainian director Serhiy Danchenko, who headed the Ivan Franko Academic Theater in Kyiv, and transferred to work with him in Kyiv. From 2001 to the last days of his life, Stupka headed the Ivan Franko Theater.

Bohdan Stupka is recognized as *Ukraine's most famous actor*. He not only had a prolific career in theater and cinema, but was also the head of the Ministry of Culture of Ukraine for two years

*Left page: Still frame from* **With Fire and Sword** *(Syrena Eg, 1999)*

# 58

# Braty Hadiukiny

Braty Hadiukinky were one of Ukraine's most successful bands in Soviet times, and they are still hugely popular today

This band was formed in Lviv in 1988 at a time when, due to Russification policies, not many Ukrainian language bands existed. They mix different genres of music, including rock 'n' roll, blues, folk, funk, and reggae. Fans immediately appreciated the band's songs for their use of irony and both Galician and Russian slang in their colloquial lyrics.

Braty Hadiukiny (Hadiukiny Brothers) had much early success in festivals and concerts both in and outside of Ukraine. However, in 1996 they stopped performing as it became in-

The name Braty Hadiukiny means Hadiukin (Viper) Brothers, and comes from a Russian children's story called *The Death of Hadiukin the Spy*. It was the group's original leader, Oleksandr Yemets, who came up with this name

Lead singer *Serhiy Kuzminskyi* passed away from throat cancer in 2009 and was buried in Lviv's Lychakiv cemeterary

Braty Hadiukiny's song "Faine Misto Ternopil" became *an unofficial hymn* of the Ukrainian city Ternopil

*Made in Ukraine, Braty Hadiukiny's fifth album*

creasingly difficult to organize concerts and technically support a nine-member band.

After a ten-year break, Braty Hadiukiny held a comeback concert in Kyiv in the winter of 2006. The concert gathered a record number of fifteen thousand fans, despite the the freezing temperatures (-28°C) outside.

The band continues to hold concerts, and in 2014 it released its first album since 1996.

In autumn 2014 and in 2015, Braty Hadiukiny went on an all-Ukraine tour to promote their new album, *Made in Ukraine*, and *to raise money for the war effort in Eastern Ukraine*

 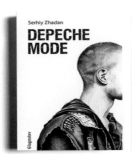 

# 59

# Serhiy Zhadan

## Upon Ukraine's independence in 1991, a new literary scene emerged from the shaky "cultural independence" of the 1990s

Writers such as Oksana Zabuzhko, Yuriy Andrukhovych, Taras Prokhasko and Andriy Kurkov have become major literary figures, both in Ukraine and internationally.

One of the most liberal and interesting representatives of Ukrainian contemporary literature is Serhiy Zhadan (born in 1974). With his books *Depeche Mode, Anarchy in the UKR, Anthem of Democratic Youth, Big Mac* and a series of poetry collections, he has voiced the yearnings of Ukrainian youth — a generation seeking personal freedom and European values, and who embraced the intellectual cultural development of an independent Ukraine.

Serhiy Zhadan's books have been translated into numerous European languages, an indication of their widespread and international appeal.

In 2018 director Yaroslav Lodygin released a film *The Wild Field* based on Serhiy Zhadan's novel Voroshylovhrad

Zhadan was the head of the tent camp in Kharkiv during *the Orange Revolution*

In addition to eight collections of poems, seven prose works, and numerous other compilations, Zhadan is also involved in different multimedia projects. He is a lead vocalist and lyrics author of the band Zhadan and the Dogs, altogether they have released four studio albums.

# 60

# Okean Elzy

## Ukraine's most internationally renowned rock band

The band Okean Elzy (which translates to Elza's Ocean) was formed in 1994 in Lviv. In 1995, the band began participating in high profile concerts and festivals in Ukraine, made its first music video and released its first unofficial single. In 1996, OE took part in a number of festivals abroad.

In 1998, OE released their first album, *Tam, de nas nema* (There, where we are not). Since that time, the band's songs have been heard continuously and everywhere in Ukraine. The band has also gained widespread popularity in Russia, even though the lyrics are sung in Ukrainian. In total, they have released nine albums.

The band's permanent front man Svyatoslav Vakarchuk is a charismatic vocalist who is highly respected by both young and old all throughout Ukraine. As a public activist and philanthropist, he is repeatedly rated as one of the most influential Ukrainians. He also holds a PhD in Physics.

Okean Elzy's lineup has changed several times. *The second permanent member of the band after Vakarchuk is the percussionist, Denys Hlinin.* The band's lineup of 1998–2004 also included guitarist Pavlo Gudimov, bass guitarist Yuriy Khustochka and keyboardist Dmytro Shurov. All of them left the band eventually to develop their own projects, including Gudimov, Esthetic Education and Pianoboy

In May 2019 Sviatoslav Vakarchuk founded *pro-European political party Voice (Holos)* to run the Ukrainian parliamentary election

Top: *Former members Denis Hlinin, Pavlo Gudimov, Svyatoslav Vakarchuk, Yurii Khustochka, Dmytro Shurov*
Bottom: *Current members Milos Jelic, Svyatoslav Vakarchuk, Vladimir Opsenica, Denis Dudko, Denis Hlinin*

It is Vakarchuk who writes most of the band's lyrics. In addition, Svyatoslav has released two solo projects, the jazz album *Vnochi* (At night) and the jazz-rock album *Brussels*, in cooperation with musicians from Okean Elzy.

Fans and music critics love Okean Elzy for their original melodies, lyricism without excessive sentimentality, unmistakable and inimical vocal style and touching lyrics. Their musical genre might be described as melodic soft rock springing from Britpop.

# 61

# PinchukArtCentre

Contemporary Ukrainian art is gaining momentum

Quite a number of Ukraine's contemporary artists have found international success — Oleksandr Hnylytskyi, Oleksandr Roytburd, Vasyl Tsaholov, Arsen Savadov, Illia Chichkan, Borys Mykhailov, Zhanna Kadyrova, and the R.E.P. group among them. The Ukrainian art scene is vibrant, with numerous galleries and centers for contemporary art. The Izolyatsia Foundation, M17 gallery, the Center for Contemporary Art, and Art Arsenal are leading arts institutions in Ukraine. But the most significant international center for contemporary art in Ukraine is the PinchukArtCentre (PAC). World-renowned Ukrainian billionaire, businessman, and philanthropist Viktor Pinchuk founded the Centre in 2006.

In 2007, Ukrainian billionaire Viktor Pinchuk became the co-owner of British artist Damien Hirst's legendary diamond skull For the Love of God that sold for *$100 million*

*Zhanna Kadyrova,* **Untitled,** *2014, Fear and Hope group exhibition*

Since its early days, the PAC has held many large-scale events — among them the retrospectives of Damien Hirst, Vik Muniz, and Sir Paul McCartney.

In 2007 and 2009, the PinchukArtCentre officially represented Ukraine at the 52nd and the 53rd Biennale in Venice — to great acclaim.

The PAC has introduced national and international awards for young artists. To profile the work of up-and-coming artists they've created the Collection Platform: Circulation — a temporary exhibition of Ukrainian and international contemporary artists.

PinchukArtCentre
address:
*1–3/2 Velyka
Vasylkivska
Street, Block A*

# 62

# Jamala

## Ukraine's winning singer at Eurovision 2016

Jamala is a Ukrainian singer and composer. She performs music that includes elements of styles such as soul, jazz, funk, folk, and electronic. She made her first professional record at the age of nine. Even though she was just a little girl, it only took a few hours to record the album of Crimean Tatar songs and songs for children.

Her debut album *For Every Heart* (2011) was released in 2011 and consists of songs she wrote herself. Jamala invented a new music style she calls "Ukrainian soul." She changes with every release, but it's always easy to recognize her, no matter what she is singing.

In her second album *All or Nothing* (2013), she recorded with a symphony orchestra and started experimenting with electronic sounds. This direction was developed in her next EP *Thank You* (2014) and her latest album *Breath* (2015).

In May 2016, Jamala won the Eurovision Song Contest with her song "1944" dedicated to the deportation of the Crimean Tatars. The world's best media, such as *the Guardian, the Washington Post, Le Monde, the New York Times,* and *Billboard* covered this story. At the moment her performance at semi-final and grand final of ESC has been watched more than twenty-one million times.

After Jamala's victory in Eurovision, the largest music label Universal Music Group got interested in her. *Jamala's album 1944 was released by Universal* *Music Group on June 10 in Europe and on July 10 in the USA.* This release features twelve compositions, eight in English and three in Ukrainian

# 63

# Odesa International Film Festival

Odesa is considered to be a city of cinema. Since 2010, it has held one of the largest International Film Festivals in Eastern Europe

The festival mainly focuses on feature-length mainstream art films. Since 2012, it has held both an international and a Ukraine-wide competition. Unlike most festivals, the Grand Prix is awarded on the basis of audience voting. The main festival prize is the Golden Duke, an updated version of the award from the eponymous Odesa Festival in 1988. Apart from the main award, the jury awards prizes for best film, best director, and best actor/actress. In the few years the festival has been running, jury chairmen have included Jos Stelling, Peter Webber, and Jerzy Stuhr.

Every summer, the festival hosts a Summer Film School, where world-class filmmakers share their knowledge while teaching master classes.

Odesa International Film Festival has issued *demands for the release of Ukrainian film director and public activist Oleg Sentsov*. In 2014 he was arrested by the Federal Security Service of the Russian Federation on suspicion of terrorism

Sentsov did not admit his guilt and called the case politically motivated and fabricated. Since the director's arrest, *protest rallies have been regularly held in a number of cities throughout Europe*

The festival also holds tribute film screenings for the directors who have contributed to the history of cinema. The most widely attended events at the festival are the open-air film screenings on the Potemkin Steps. One of the most popular shows was held in 2015 — it was *Man with a Movie Camera* screened to the musical accompaniment of Michael Nyman's neoclassical minimalist orchestra.

# FOOD

# 64

# Bread

For an agricultural nation with old traditions, bread is more than just food — it symbolizes life and the sun. It is a gift from God

Bread has always been the main protection charm that ensures the sanctity of Ukrainian homes. No holiday, ritual, or important event is complete without it. Traditionally, people take bread to birthdays, greet their guests with it, and use it to bless newlyweds during weddings. Bread even accompanies the departed as they transition from this world to the next.

Even in pre-Christian times bread was considered a deity. Gods were disgusted with slaughtered animals' blood, and for this reason, food, and primarily bread, became the main object of sacrifice. In Christianity, bread symbolizes the body of Christ. But beyond its religious connotations for an ordinary Ukrainian, a loaf of bread is respected for the sustenance it brings. Earlier generations of Ukrainians lived with the constant fear of famine. Horrific events such as the Holodomor (man-made famine) of the 1930s have instilled a great respect for food,

*Traditional black Ukrainian bread*

When Ukraine's disgraced president fled his palatial grounds on the outskirts of Kyiv, he left behind a solid gold loaf of bread

This *"golden baton"* has become a symbol of his regime's corruption

especially bread. Throwing away a piece of bread is considered sacrilege to this day.

Ukrainian ethnographers have gathered accounts of more than eighty kinds of ritual bread in Ukraine! Two great Ukrainian clas-sics are the black "Ukrainian bread" and the white "baton." Ukrainian bakeries have a wide selection of breads — all are worth trying.

Ukraine's rich dark soil and the vast fields of wheat have earned it the nickname "bread basket" of Europe.

# 65

# Korovai

## Korovai is a round holiday bread made of white wheat

Ukrainians greet their dear guests with "bread and salt" or a korovai with a pinch of salt on a festive embroidered *rushnyk*. This custom originates from pagan times, when bread was considered to be of divine nature.

*Korovais* are baked on big holidays, and especially for weddings. Several rituals accompany the process of baking korovai. It must be prepared by an uneven number of happily married women, and a curly-haired boy must be the one to place the bread in the oven.

Rich and embellished with baked dough ornaments and kalyna branches, Korovai has always been the main decoration on wedding tables. The bread is to be cut by the godfather of the groom or the bride. The topmost portion of the bread, with wheat cones and birds, would be given to the newly married couple, the middle to the guests, and the lower part with coins usually baked into it would go to the wedding musicians.

In honor of
the twentieth
anniversary
of Ukraine's
Independence,
*a record-breaking
1.5 ton and 4x4
meter Korovai*
was baked in
Vinnytsia! 1,000
kg flour, 350 liters
of milk, 2,000
eggs, 175 kg of
sugar and many
other ingredients
were used in its
production

# 66

# Hrechka

Buckwheat, the grain which once became
a symbol of electoral fraud in Ukraine

A porridge made from the buckwheat grain — *hrechka* — is
one of Ukraine's national dishes, usually served with a knob
of butter and a pinch of salt. Hrechka can also be served as a
side dish with meat or fish, or can be a base for soups. It's also
an essential ingredient during the Lenten fast, with people
making fritters out of it called *hrechanyky*.

The buckwheat plant is grown throughout Ukraine.
People also make honey out of buckwheat, and this honey
is noted for its rich dark-brown color. Buckwheat is also
praised for its high nutritional content, and is packed full of
vitamins and minerals.

In Ukraine, hrechka's cultural value is almost more important than its culinary one. At the beginning of the 2010s, it
became a symbol of electoral corruption; political parties would

The saying
*"to jump in
the hrechka"*
means to betray
someone, or
have premarital
relations

dole out free food to potential voters, with hrechka the main product they would be giving to people. As a result the price of buckwheat soared, and politicians were accused of currying favor by "sowing the electorate with hrechka."

During the majority candidate elections in Chernihiv in 2015, one of the candidates earned himself the nickname "Marshal Hrechka" for the sheer amount of hrechka he was giving away. However, the citizens of Chernihiv started to get smart with the politicians, queueing up several times for free food or even selling it afterward. This form of indirect bribery with the help of hrechka has already fallen out of fashion, with electoral candidates resorting to more traditional campaigns, such as building children's playgrounds and schools, to win votes.

Still used until relatively recent times, one of the severest punishments for children was *to make them kneel on uncooked hrechka grains*

# 67

# Horilka

## This famous alcoholic drink is nicknamed "okovyta" by Ukrainians and Poles

The term *horilka* is derived from the Latin *aqua vitae*, or "water of life." For Slavs, horilka is a cult drink. Ancient residents of warmer lands, such as the ancient Greeks and Romans, considered any drink stronger than wine to be barbarian. But life in harsher climes dictates more severe conditions of survival and different gastronomic tastes — hence a Slavic preference for the strong brew.

Researchers suppose that horilka was invented sometime in the twelfth and the thirteenth centuries. The invention of this "bread wine" is attributed to poor peasants who,

Horilka is also made with *honey, mint, or even milk.* In some cases whole red peppers are put into the bottle. It is then named horilka with pepper, or pertsivka. A rare type of horilka is even distilled from nettle!

*Still frame from Soviet film **The Lost Letter** (Dovzhenko Film Studios, 1972)*

looking for a cheap alternative to mead, were forced to use less expensive grain crops as a base ingredient.

Horilka manufacturing appeared in Ukraine in the time of the Zaporizhian Sich. Kozaks valued Ukrainian horilka over other alcoholic drinks and even exported it to Russia. Despite a strict dry law during military campaigns, many kozaks are thought to have bent this regulation and continued on with their horilka-induced merriment.

A night of horilka drinking will surely lead to a lot of fun — but drink with moderation. It's potent stuff!

The home-distilled horilka, popular in the villages, is called *samohon* (literally "self-run," "self-destilled")

# 68

# Salo

The French have foie gras, Ukrainians have salo — a traditional food made of salted pork fat

The importance of this popular Ukrainian food dates back to the Tatar-Mongol period. Over several centuries, Tatar-Mongols periodically attacked ancient Ukrainians, taking them prisoner and capturing their cattle. For religious reasons, the Muslim occupiers had no interest in consuming pork.

Hence, it became a useful food for survival in hard times.

To visit Kyiv without trying authentic Ukrainian salo (pork fatback) is tantamount to a crime! To find the best salo in the city be sure to drop by the centrally located Bessarabska Market. Further afield, the Zhytnii and Volody-

*Left page:* **Salo in chocolate** *is a special Ukrainian treat*

Check out the For a delicious salo tasting session check out the Bessarabka market at *z Bessarabska Square* for a delicious salo tasting session!

For preservation, salo is salted and sometimes also smoked and aged in a dark and cold place, where it will *last for a year or more*

myrsky markets also have a fine selection.

Picking out salo is a true art. It should be white, with a pinkish shade. The most tender pieces come from the back and the sides of a pig. Some people prefer "general's salo" — salo with more meat. At Kyiv markets you can find raw, salted or smoked, herbed, or spiced salo. You can eat it on its own; chop it and add it to borscht (beetroot soup) or on top of *varenyky* (dumplings); or have it sliced on rye bread, rubbed with garlic, along with a shot of horilka. There are many ways to enjoy this tasty treat.

# 69

# Porcini Mushroom

The heroes of fairy tales and a favorite ingredient during the Lent fasting period: he is called the king of mushrooms

Porcini or *borovyky* mushrooms: large and fragrant, these mushrooms are a real find for mushroom pickers, who hunt for them throughout summer and autumn. You measure the success of a mushroom-hunting trip by the amount of white mushrooms you find, since they are considered the noblest (and most expensive) kind. Its name — white — comes from the way the mushroom retains its color, even after cutting, cooking, and drying.

White mushrooms are an integral part of Ukrainian cuisine. At Lent, when people traditionally abstain from meat, Ukrainians tend to add them to borsch or hrechka; they also make sauces and soups, fry them, or marinate them for winter. However, the most popular way of preserving them is to dry them. Every Ukrainian is familiar with the sight of a row of dried white mushrooms being sold at the market or on roadsides, where you can buy them on your way back home from the countryside. In the Carpathians, gathering mushrooms ("silent hunting") is a favorite pastime, and local mushroom pickers and amateur tourists compete to find them.

*Old Man Borovichok* is a character in children fairy tales, a mythological guardian of nature and the forest. He's known by the majority of Ukrainians as the hero of the Soviet film Morozko, directed by Oleksandr Rou in the 1960s

# 70

# Eggplant Caviar

This classic Odesa appetizer with Greek and Jewish roots is referred to as "blue caviar" by the locals

As with forshmak and sprat fish cakes, there are dozens of options in Odesa for making eggplant caviar. Besides caviar, eggplant is prepared in many other ways, such as stewing it in cream sauce, cooking it with onions, or even preparing it with jam.

The basis of the eggplant caviar recipe is a blackened baked eggplant, from which the rind is removed. It is then finely chopped with a knife and mixed with tomatoes, garlic, onions, herbs, black pepper, and sunflower oil in a deep bowl and left to cool. It is often served as a snack or spread on bread with salted cheese. Some recipes call for baked bell peppers, and others use olive oil instead of sunflower.

In his memoirs, the famous Odesan writer Valentyn Katayev wrote that baked eggplant should only be cut with a wooden knife. This is because the blue color of the eggplant is lost when it comes into contact with metal. Therefore, according to some, this is the only way to make the authentic recipe.

Eggplant caviar was very common in the USSR, and its popularity was played out in the famous Soviet comedy *Ivan Vasilievich*

After joking about *overseas caviar being made out of eggplants*, it became a popular dish

# 71

# Varenyky

Crescent-shaped pockets of dough which
are stuffed then boiled — a national favorite

The *varenyky* recipe was most likely borrowed from Turkish *dyushvara* and modified to fit our tastes. Varenyky are commonly made using a yeastless dough from wheat flour. There are a variety of fillings, but cherries, cottage cheese, potatoes and cracklings are most popular with Ukrainians. The main dish is usually served with sour cream or fried onions. Sweet varenyky are sprinkled with sugar and flavored with honey and syrups.

Varenyky play a significant role in Ukrainian folklore and are linked to a number of folk traditions. Ancient Ukrainians believed that eating varenyky on certain days contributed to their good fortune; girls would use varenyky for fortune-telling; new mothers would be offered the dish after undergoing labor. The varenyky's form is reminiscent of a crescent moon — an important symbol for many ancient Ukrainians' beliefs.

*A monument to varenyky* portraying a happy Cossack with a full pot of varenyky was unveiled in Cherkasy in 2006

*Stillframes from the Soviet film **Evenings on a Farm Near Dikanka** (Kinostudiya imeni Gorkogo, 1961)*

# 72

# Borsch

## Hearty, with perfect complements of sweet and sour, Ukrainian borsch is not to be missed

The dish originated with oxalic broth made by primitive people on the Ukrainian territories and, after many centuries, has transformed into the contemporary "green borsch." The majority of linguists opine that the word *borsch* derives from the name of a wild plant. Cow parsley or *borschivnyk*, as well as beetroot, have both grown on Ukrainian lands for ages. Together they were the main ingredients of the ancient "red borsch" in Kyiv Rus.

For a Ukrainian, contemporary borsch is a cult dish. There are at least thirty traditional recipes for borsch. Borsch can be served hot or cold; red or green; based on meat or mushroom broth; sweet or sour; with salo, kvas, or fish; with grain or flour products like *halushky* and *vushky*. Everyone makes it their own way — as the saying goes: a thousand hostesses, a thousand borsches! True or not, borsch remains the main dish on the tables of the majority of Ukrainian families. While it's eaten daily, it's also eaten on holidays, sometimes at weddings and always at wakes.

Borsch with lots of pepper was used to test young kozaks' endurance at *Zaporizhian Sich*.

Non-beet varieties of borsch also exist, such as the tomato-paste-based *orange borsch*, popular in eastern Ukraine, and *green borsch* (sorrel soup) often enjoyed in the summer.

# 73

# Beer

## Beer needs no introduction. It is mankind's most ancient drink

The history of brewing dates back thousands of years: ancient Egyptians possessed a recipe for making barley malt, and Sumerians were known to have brewed over fifteen kinds of beer. Archaeological excavations in Kyiv have shown that commercial beer brewing has a long history here as well — there is evidence of such activities taking place during the reign of Yaroslav the Wise (983–1054). The production of malt (as it was called at the time) was not only an occupation for townspeople. It was also a monastic activity.

Today Ukrainian beer has become famous, with many brands winning international accolades for their quality and superior taste. A wide variety of beer brands are offered on the Ukrainian market and for export. Ukraine also has many microbreweries that produce a range of signature beers, offering a great deal of variety.

There are more than *forty local breweries* in Ukraine

Some of the most renowned Ukrainian beers are *Chernihivske, Obolon, Lvivske, and Berdychivske*

*Taranka* is a traditional cured fish, usually from the carp family, eaten with beer

Beer is a popular choice of drink for *a date night*

Given the quality and diversity of Ukrainian beer, many think the country could develop beer tourism similar to that of Germany and the Czech Republic.

As you discover the many fine beers Ukraine has to offer, don't forget about moderation. Ukrainian legislation considers beer an alcoholic drink.

# 74

# Banosh

## A delectable dish, most commonly found in the Carpathian region of Ukraine

It is cooked with corn flour, sour cream, cream, and a small amount of water. It is served with *brynza* cheese, crackling, cottage cheese, or mushrooms.

Banosh (or *tokan*) was traditionally made by Carpathian shepherds. Sheep breeding was a male occupation and according to mountaineers' customs, banosh, as well as brynza, must be made exclusively by men. In contemporary times, this rule is neglected as much as the essential condition that real banosh must be cooked on an open fire. Never mind the compromises, the majority of restaurants or, rather, *kolybas* in Carpathian Ukraine will gladly treat tourists to this seemingly simple but truly incomparable dish.

The closest "relative" of banosh is *kulesha*, or *mamalyga*. It is also based on corn flour, but does not include sour cream. It may be familiar to you as italian polenta.

Traditionally, banosh is cooked by boiling *water, salt, cornmeal, and sour cream* in a special-shaped cast-iron pot

# 75

# Kholodets

Jellied meat — an essential part
of festive winter meals

The stock can be made of beef, pork, lamb, or chicken. This dish is usually served with mustard or horseradish.

*Kholodets* is one of Ukraine's most popular national dishes. It originates from the northern regions of Europe and Russia. In the olden days, during long travel and military campaigns, you would make a bowl of stock that in low temperatures would set to a gelatinous consistency. Though this dish originated in northern regions, it gained popularity with Slavic people, and most notably, Ukrainians.

Kholodets connoisseurs assert that each region of Ukraine makes its own kholodets. It's said that the tastiest kholodets is made from a rooster and has very little fat.

The dish gets its name from kholod, *the Ukrainian word for cold*. While it's commonly consumed in the winter, it can be cooked anytime — as long as you have a few hours to spare. It's not a quick meal!

Kholodets stock is made from *meat and bones* (usually pork). Upon cooling, the liquid congeals because of the natural gelatin found in the bones

Kholodets is usually eaten with *horseradish*, which is usually red in Ukraine, because it is mixed with beetroot

Truly delicious kholodets is made with *rooster meat*

# 76

# Kyiv Cake

This mouthwatering cake of the capital can be found anywhere

Layers of crunchy meringue that melts in your mouth, surrounded by buttercream frosting and hazelnut chunks throughout — you won't find another cake like it! It's no wonder this is a favorite souvenir for visitors to bring back to their friends and family. You'll find pyramids of the white cake boxes with green chestnut leaves at Kyiv's Central Railway Station and Zhuliany or Boruspil International Airports — all ready for the trek home.

In 2016, Kyiv cake celebrated its sixtieth anniversary. The recipe is said to have been invented thanks to a serendipitous mistake made by confectioners of the former Karl Marx Confectionary Factory (recently renamed Roshen). Today, the confectionary factory Roshen remains the leader in producing Kyiv cake — making around fifteen tons of the cake per night!

The recipe of Kyiv cake's layers and cream is *a commercial secret*

*Leonid Brezhnev* was known to have a sweet tooth for Kyiv cake. For the general secretary's seventieth birthday, the Kyiv factory created a special seventy-piece cake

# 77

# Chicken Kyiv

Pounded chicken breast, wrapped in butter and herbs, breaded and deep fried — simply divine

The ideal Chicken Kyiv has a crisp fried shell with garlicky butter on the inside. Food lovers suggest two alternative modes of preparation. Old-fashioned recipes involve pounding the butter into the breast with a cooking hammer, giving the meat a tender creamy taste. Or you can wrap the butter (mixed with garlic and herbs) in chicken. Cheese, mushrooms, and greens can also be added to the filling.

*A classic chicken Kyiv* is made with a chicken breast with the wing still attached

The origins of this dish are a matter of debate. Russians believe the dish was created in the 1970s for the opening of Kyiv's Moscow Hotel. A Ukrainian hotelier quoted in the *New York Times* dates the dish to 1819. The *Russian Tea Room Cookbook* credits Chicken Kyiv to the renowned French chef Careme at the Court of Alexander I. The food historian Vilyam Pokhlebkin also dates it to the Tsarist regime.

Origins aside, this breaded, boneless chicken cutlet, cooked stuffed with butter and herbs, is a hugely popular dish. It's ubiquitous in its namesake capital... you'll find it on the menu at cheap fast food outlets and fancy restaurants alike. When you order the dish, just don't cut into it with your knife! Hot melted butter can squirt out and burn you, or at the very least make a big mess. Instead, pierce the dish with your fork, wait until the butter drips out, and enjoy.

# 78

# Krovianka

One of Ukraine's most peculiar dishes

Its preparation is complicated, yet lovers of "blood sausage" think the result well worth the effort.

During a pig's slaughter, the animals' large intestines are saved and processed. After a thorough cleaning, they are stuffed with a filling made of grain, minced meat, raw pig blood, onions, salo, milk-soaked bread, and spices. Stuffed krovianka can be boiled and fried or smoked. In the days before refrigeration, this sausage covered in lard could be kept in a cool place for a long time.

This dish is also made in the Spanish province of Galicia and in Scotland. Scots use sheep stomachs instead of pig intestines for stuffing. This traditional Scottish dish is called *haggis*.

Krovianka is not the most attractive-looking food, but to gastronomic connoisseurs, it's *a real treat*

Returning to Ukrainians, it is necessary to note that they always have been great lovers of *krovianka* despite religious prohibition to consume the blood of slaughtered animals. Religious controversy has ended, with recipes for blood sausage surviving to the present day.

*Homemade krovianka abound at Ukrainian markets*

Krovianka is usually made before Christmas or Easter for the holiday meal, but guests of Ukraine can find it on the menus of many restaurants specializing in Ukrainian cuisine. We also recommend you try other kinds of homemade sausage. Bon appetit!

# PLACES

*Right page:* **The Motherland Monument**, *Kyiv*

# 79

# Trypillia

## At the end of the nineteenth century, archaeologist Vikentiy Khvoika discovered severa Neolithic settlements on Ukrainian territory

One such settlement was located on the outskirts of the small town of Trypillia in Kyiv Oblast. This finding led to international archaeological recognition for the little town.

Trypillian culture was far-reaching — it encompassed the territories of modern-day Ukraine, Romania, and Moldova. From the second half of 6,000 BC to the first centuries of 3,000 BC, the biggest settlements in Europe belonged to

Address of the
National Museum
of the History
of Ukraine:
*2 Volodymyrska
Street, Kyiv*

*During the excavation of a Trypillia village Odaiv II*

this culture. Archaeological evidence shows that this group practiced agriculture, pottery, weaving, and metalwork, thus surpassing many other civilizations of that time.

Contemporary researchers have found cause to link many of Ukraine's cultural inheritances to its Trypillian forebears. These influences are evident in modern-day religious beliefs, elements of folklore, and traditional crafts. There remains much to be learned about this ancient civilization and its legacies.

A private museum dedicated entirely to Trypillian culture has recently been opened in the village bearing its name. The museum popularizes the notion that Ukrainians derive from Trypillians. Trypillian history is also featured in the National Museum of the History of Ukraine.

Address of the private Historical and Archaeological Museum "Ancient Aratta — Ukraine": *1 Rybolovetska Street, Trypillia, Kyiv Oblast*

# 80

# St. Sophia Cathedral

The oldest building in the city and the oldest Christian church on the lands of the East Slavs to have survived to the present day

Prince Yaroslav the Wise founded this cathedral at the beginning of the eleventh century. Since that time, Sophia Kyivska has survived dozens of Tatar-Mongol raids, multiple destructions and fires. Even nine centuries later, after numerous restorations and renovations, this cathedral was harmed once more, having been looted first by the Soviet authorities and then later by its Nazi occupiers. Today, the rebuilt cathedral is a designated UNESCO World Heritage site.

You can visit the Sophia Kyivska at *24 Volodymyrska Street*

The St. Sophia Cathedral contains breathtaking eleventh-century mosaics. They embellish the altar and the central domes. The six-meter mosaic image of Oranta (Virgin Mary) is extraordinary. Observed from different locations in the cathedral, she appears in different poses. Be sure to check out the ancient frescoes from the eleventh to eighteenth centuries. The cathedral's grounds also house a necropolis — a burial place for prominent Ukrainian historical and religious leaders.

The St. Sophia Cathedral is without a doubt a unique masterpiece of Ukrainian architecture. It's one of the main cultural and religious centers of Orthodox Christianity and one of the most frequently visited tourist attractions in Eastern Europe.

The Virgin Orans, Oranta (the Great Panagia) is a well-known Orthodox Christian depiction of the Virgin Mary in prayer with extended arms. *The six-meter-high mosaic* is located in the vault of the chancel. The icon is original to the cathedral — present since its foundation by Yaroslav the Wise in the twelfth century

# 81

# Khersones

One of the most ancient cities on the territory of modern Ukraine (today it is a part of Sevastopol)

Khersones was founded in the south of the Crimean peninsula in 422 BC as a Greek colony. At first, it was a highly developed city-state that even minted its own coin. At the same time, Khersones's location on the crossroads of many trade routes made it a prize for invaders. The history of this city is mainly a succession of defensive wars, devastation, and destruction. The final strike that Khersones didn't manage to survive was in 1399. The Golden Horde commander Edigu invaded Khersones and burnt it to the ground.

Today the National Museum-Reserve "Khersones Tavriyskyi" is situated on the site of the former city. Here you can walk the once crowded blocks of the ancient city, see the remains of the ancient theater, defensive walls of the fortress, marble columns of the basilica, and more. But since 2014 the Crimean peninsula — and Khersones along with it — has been illegally occupied by Russia, so it is uneasy get there.

Address of the National Museum-Reserve "Khersones Tavriyskyi" is *1 Drevnia Street, Sevastopol, Crimea*

Khersones is included on the international list of historic and archaeological places that *suffer the most from tourists*

# 82

# Baturyn

## A small city in the north of Ukraine, but once an important Hetman capital

While Baturyn is a quiet town today, in the seventeenth through eighteenth centuries it was the main residence of Ukrainian hetmans. The area prospered and grew under the rule of Hetman Ivan Mazepa (1639–1709). It was then sacked by the Russian army in 1708 and then rebuilt again under the leadership of Hetman Kyrylo Rozumovskyi — though it would never regain its former glory.

Today, you can get a glimpse of the town's past by visiting the historical and cultural reserve of the "Hetmans' Capital." You can visit the old citadel, Rozumovskyi's Palace (built in 1799–1803) and the Intercession Church.

A number of archaeological excavations are presently being carried out in and around the town. These places are immensely rich with artifacts from the Kozak era. This isn't surprising considering that, during its heyday under Hetman Mazepa, more than twenty thousand people lived here — kozak noblemen among them.

Under Hetman *Ivan Mazepa* (eft page) Baturyn boasted forty churches and chapels, two monasteries, and a college for government officials and diplomats

The national historical and cultural reserve Hetman's Capital includes *thirty-nine historical and archeological monuments*

*Bottom: Palace of Hetman Kyrylo Rozumovskyi, built 1799–1803*

# 83

# Dilove Village

## Ukrainians like to think that the center of Europe is in fact a Ukrainian village

Determining Europe's geographic center is an exercise in relativity, so it is not a surprise that a number of hypothetical centers, located in entirely different places, exist today. One of the most well-known is situated near the village of Dilove, Zakarpattia Oblast, Ukraine.

At the end of nineteenth century a sign was placed here proclaiming it to be "the Center of Europe." It carries an inscription in Latin which translates to: "A permanent, precise, and eternal place. The center of Europe was determined very precisely, with an apparatus created in Austria-Hungary according to the scale of meridians and parallels, in the year 1887." The measurement was performed by Austrian land surveyors. Later, Soviet scientists confirmed their findings.

People joke that every European country claims to have a geographic center of Europe. In any case, Dilove has become a tourist attraction. Stop by and snap a photo next to the famous sign, admire picturesque landscapes, and treat yourself to a tasty Hutsul meal in the local *kolyba*-museum.

# 84

# Olesko Castle

## Ukraine, especially its western part, used to be at the heart of Europe's political and military battles

Abundant warfare in Ukrainian lands led to the construction of many fortresses and castles. Unfortunately, few have survived to this day. One of the most famous is Olesko Castle, situated in Lviv Oblast.

This landmark, built and rebuilt between the thirteenth and eighteenth centuries, is architectural landmark that annually attracts thousands of tourists from all over Ukraine. The Lviv Art Gallery has taken over a wing of the castle — in it you'll find a great collection of medieval furniture, old Polish portraits, tapestries, Ukrainian icons, and even instruments of torture!

Over its long life the castle has been hit by lightning and was once partially destroyed during an earthquake. It has housed a women's school, barracks, and military storage and has gone through cycles of neglect, disrepair, and restoration. Today the castle has been revived thanks in large part to the academic Borys Voznytskyi (1926– 2012), who is nicknamed the "guardian angel" of Ukrainian museums and castles.

The famous Polish King *Jan III Sobieski* was born in Olesko Castle in 1629

*34 Zamkova Street, Olesko, Lviv Oblast*

*Left page: **Portrait of Jan III Sobieski**, Jan Styka 1858–1925*

# 85

# The Lychakiv Cemetery

## The history of Lviv is carved in this cemetery's stones

The Lychakiv Cemetery is the oldest burial ground in the city that's still in use. It was created in 1786 following a ban on burials in church graveyards.

Today, this cemetery is not only a place of eternal rest for the deceased or just a landscaped park with beautiful old trees and well-arranged alleys. It is also like an open-air museum of memorial sculptures and architecture.

The oldest gravestone here dates back to the seventeenth century, though there are few gravestones from that time. Only a small number that date back to before the mid-nineteenth century have survived to this day. This is due to the installment of a stone crusher at that time, and the decision to crush any gravestones that nobody had taken care of for more than twenty-five years. The crushed stones were used to pave the cemetery's alleys.

There are more than three hundred thousand graves at this cemetery. Many of the crypts and tombstones are true works of art, such as the sculpture on the gravestone of actress Regina Markovska (known as "Sleeping Beauty"). Also noteworthy is the tombstone of the Armenian archbishop Stefanovych featuring elements of traditional Armenian sacral architecture.

You can trace the history of Lviv and Galicia by the names of those buried at the cemetery. Most of Lviv's outstanding politicians, scientists, writers, and artists rest in peace here.

Today, the Lychakiv Cemetery is not only a graveyard, but also an official museum. You can order a tour on the cemetery's website at *www.lviv-lychakiv.ukrain.travel*

The Lychakiv Cemetery has its own legends. The most romantic is a story about *the Polish artist Artur Grottger and his fiancé Wanda Monné*. They never married due to the artist's illness and subsequent death in France. Monné sold all her jewelry and a part of her dowry to bring her beloved one back to Lviv to bury him in the Lychakiv Cemetery in accordance with his will. Legend has it that the ghosts of Artur and Wanda can sometimes be seen wandering in the moonlight

Lviv's multicultural heritage is felt even at this cemetery, where you can find Polish, Ukrainian, German, and Armenian names on the tombstones.

Even to this day, the most prominent residents of Lviv are buried in Lychakiv cemetery; however, nowadays this is quite rare.

# 86

# The Motherland Monument

A massive female warrior stands guard over Kyiv

On Victory Day of May 9, 1981, the general secretary of the Communist Party — Leonid Brezhnev — unveiled "The Motherland". Original plans would have seen this monument gold-plated. But even the Soviet fondness for monumentalism had its limits, so the sculpture was fashioned instead out of stainless steel. Separate parts weighing several dozens of tons each were welded at the Paris Commune plant in Kyiv.

The Motherland Monument is a part of the Museum of the Great Patriotic War complex found at *44 Ivana Mazepy Street*

In the end, the sculpture came to weigh around 450 tons. Together with its pedestal, it reaches to 102 meters. The steel woman brandishes a 9-ton sword in her right hand and 13-ton and 13×8-meter shield in her left.

Two elevators function inside of the sculpture. You can also climb the stairs up to the sword and shield where you'll find an observation deck.

"The Motherland" faces toward Moscow. Kyivans joke that she defends against Russians, a joke that has taken on new meaning during this time of war.

# 87

# Pyrohiv

## You can go back in time with a visit to this vast open-air historical museum

Near the village of Pyrohiv, on the southern outskirts of Kyiv, you'll find the biggest open-air ethnographic museum in Europe. Here you can see over three hundred unique buildings from the sixteenth to the twentieth centuries. The museum opened for visitors in 1976, after its curators spent seven whole years collecting historical structures from across Ukraine.

The National Museum of Folk Architecture and Life of Ukraine has res-idential houses from various regions of the country, windmills and watermills, churches, barns, a school, a tavern, a village council, and other buildings. Meandering through its pastoral grounds takes you back in time. If you take a guided tour, you'll be able to see many of the interiors of the buildings as well — giving you a sense of what life was like for peasants centuries ago.

Every weekend, the museum hosts various festivals where you

The setting for the National Museum of Folk Architecture and Life of Ukraine is the bucolic countryside. You can spend the whole day here *picnicking and exploring its numerous walking trails*

National holidays — Christian and ancient pagan alike — are observed at the Museum. Plan a visit during these times and join in the celebrations! To see what's on, go to: *www.pyrohiv. com.ua/en*

The museum is also *a popular place to get married*. Couples can choose to get married in one of a variety of churches from different regions of Ukraine

can learn national crafts from master craftsmen, taste traditional dishes, and enjoy Ukrainian singing and dancing. The museum also occa-sionally organizes thematic exhibitions — there are over seventy thousand rare display units with unique icons, embroidery, dishes, and tools.

# 88

# Chornobyl

## Chornobyl has come to be associated the world over with scenes of devastation and destruction

A few decades ago no one would have thought that the name of one of Ukraine's very ordinary and picturesque towns would be engraved in world history and in the memory of Ukrainian people, with heavy black letters. Until the explosion at Nuclear Power Plant Fukushima-1 in Japan in 2011, it was considered the biggest disaster in the history of nuclear energy.

On April 26, 1986, reactor number four of the Chornobyl nuclear power plant, situated in Kyiv Oblast of the former Ukrainian SSR, exploded and spewed a vast amount of radioactive substances into the atmosphere. Radioactive smoke drifted over the northern part of Ukraine, Belarus, and a number of European countries — reaching as far as the eastern USA. At first the authorities of the Ukrainian SSR and the USSR tried to conceal the scale of the tragedy, but this proved to be an impossible task. Soon, evacuation from

Viktor Marushchenko was one of the first to take photos of the Chornobyl disaster. The photo is foggy with bright spots in the lower half due to high levels of radiation

Many Kyiv companies offer tours to Chernobyl, where one will undoubtedly be impressed by the desolation and natural beauty of the Polissya region. You can order a tour to Chornobyl at www. chornobyl-tour.ua

In May 2019 HBO released a miniseries that depicts the Chernobyl nuclear disaster

the most polluted regions began. In total, approximately six hundred thousand people suffered radiation damage. First responders experienced horrifying effects, and many died in agony.

A thirty-kilometer exclusion zone was created around the pow-er plant. In the absence of people, wildlife in this zone is flourishing, though it's unclear how the radiation is affecting them. Some people penetrate these boundaries, with tours offered of the eerie, abandoned place — a grotesque memorial to human error and folly.

# 89

# The Potemkin Steps

## Thanks to the famous film The Battleship Potemkin by Sergei Eisenstein, the Potemkin Steps are internationally renowned

The film's action takes place in Odesa in 1905 during the mutiny of the eponymous ship. A baby carriage rolling down the enormous set of stairs, people escaping in panic — these famous shots were significant not only for the film, but brought fame to the shoot's location.

The Steps were designed by architect Francesco Boffo in 1825 and were built by the engineers Upton and Morozov in 1841. They unite the center of Odesa with the Odesa Marine Station and harbor. Amounting to 192 steps (originally there were 200), the stairs measure 142 meters in length, making them among the longest in Europe.

After Ukrainian independence in 1991, the Potemkin Steps, like many streets in Odesa, were given back their original name, *the Prymorski Stairs*. But locals still know and refer to the stairs by their Soviet name

*Left page: Poster for the 1905 silent film* **The Battleship Potemkin** *(Mosfilm)*

The lower section of the steps is almost twice as wide as the upper section — creating a visual illusion that they have the same width from beginning to end.

Despite the great number of stairs, they are easy to climb. They were built at an optimal angle so pedestrians don't strain their legs.

In the nineteenth century, the steps were called the Giant Staircase; later, they were known as the Richelieu and Boulevard steps. It was only in 1955 that the staircase was renamed the Potemkin Steps in honor of the fiftieth anniversary of the mutiny of Battleship Potemkin.

Curiously, a person looking down the stairs *sees only the landings,* and the steps are invisible, but a person looking up *sees only steps,* and the landings are invisible

# 90

# Livadiya

The Livadiya architectural park complex is Yalta's main attraction and one of the most interesting tourist destinations in Ukraine

Livadiya (from the Greek *meadow*) has a long history of settlement since the Bronze Age. After Crimea became a part of Russia, Livadiya changed ownership several times before being finally bought by the tsar's family. The complex became the tsar's summer residence with all the imperial privileges — orchards and greenhouses, a park with valuable species of subtropical plants, hotbeds, an ice-producing plant, and a winter theater.

The biggest attraction of the Livadiya complex is the Great White Palace, built in the Italian Renaissance style using white stone produced near Inkerman. There are many other attractions on the site — the Italian patio, the Palace's Exaltation of the Holy Cross Church, a house that belonged to the minister of the court, Baron Frederick, and the tsar's Path or Sunny Path that leads from Livadiya Park to Gaspra.

On 18 March 2014 Russia formally annexed Crimea, so currently it is not easy to visit.

On February 4, 1945, the Yalta Conference convened in Livadiya Palace. It was here that the Big Three — *Stalin, Roosevelt, and Churchill* — decided the fate of Europe

It is said that in the event of Nazi occupation, *Hitler* had planned to give the White Palace to Goering

*Left page: Ivan Aivazovsky,* **View from Livadia,** *1861*

# 91

# Bakhchysarai

The former capital of the Crimean Khanate and the former administrative center of the Crimean Tatars

Bakhchysarai is situated at the foot of steep cliffs in the Churuk-Su River valley. The area has a remarkably long history of settlement stretching back more than forty thousand years! An astonishing eighty-thousand-year-old paleolithic settlement has been found nearby. Taurians, Scythians, Greeks, Alans, Goths, Sarmatians, Huns, Khazars, and Pechenegs — all of them left their mark on this area. The Crimean Khanate, for example, created a "Garden Palace" (or Bakhchysarai). Today the Crimean peninsula — and Bakhchysarai along with it — has been illegally occupied by Russia.

Visitors to this unique city can enjoy ancient monuments such as the remains of the cave fortress city Chufut-Kale, the palace of Crimean khans — Khansaray, the Fountain of Tears in the Khan Palace, and a number of ancient mosques.

The biggest Turkic cemetery in Europe is situated not far from *Chufut-Kale*. Karaites were buried here for more than 1,500 years. The majority of inscriptions preserved on gravestones are in Aramaic — the language of the Bible. The number of Karaite graves in this cemetery vastly outnumbers the current population of Karaites

*The As-sumption Monastery* of the Caves, dating back to the fifteenth century

# 92

# Uman

## A major pilgrimage site for Breslov Hasidic Jews

Located between Kyiv and Odesa, Uman is best known among Ukrainians for its depiction of the *haidamak* (a sort of Kozak military band) rebellion in Taras Shevchenko's *Haidamaky* and as a piligrimage site for Breslov Hasidic Jews.

Uman is home to the grave of the Jewish spiritual leader Rebbe Nachman, the founder of the Breslov movement, who died there in 1810. The Jews believe that on his deathbed Rebbe Nachman said that all those who visited his grave on Rosh Hashanah would be freed from stress and suffering and have a good year ahead. So since the 1990s, in the days and weeks leading up to Rosh Hashanah, Breslov Hasidim from around the world — mostly from New York, Israel, the UK, and Canada — travel to Uman.

Though Uman is a small town (eighty thousand residents), it has a growing Jewish population, mostly involved in providing services to Jewish tourists. Rosh Hashanah in Uman has become a veritable institution, with exuberant dancing, often compared to a Hasidic Burning Man.

The site was a major Jewish pilgrimage spot before the Russian Revolution and Civil War, and became so again *after the Soviet Union collapsed in 1991*

After the Second World War, a Breslov Hasid managed *to locate the Rebbe's grave and preserved it* when the Soviets turned the entire area into a housing project

# 93

# Sofiyivka

## Half a million people visit this peaceful paradise yearly; it's also a research institute of the National Academy of Sciences of Ukraine

The Polish noble Stanislaw Stanisław *Szczęsny* Potocki built the Sofiyivka park in the Ukrainian town of Uman in 1796 — it's named in honor of his beloved wife Sofia. The project was conceived and overseen by the military engineer Ludwik Metzel, who masterfully combined natural landscape with artificial architectural elements such as pools, grottos, waterfalls, gazebos, and sculpture. This beauty flourishes thanks to the two-hundred-meter underground river Acheron which feeds the Great Waterfalls.

In the more than two hundred years since the park's establishment, it has changed owners several times. Over time, new buildings, pavilions, and landscape features have been incorporated. Today Sofiyivka is one of the main dendrological parks in Ukraine. It encompasses an area of 179 hectares with more than 2,000 species of local and exotic trees.

Guided tours are available daily, and there are a variety of souvenir shops and cafes on the grounds. Visitors are welcome to ride gondolas and catamarans on the park's rivers.

The park is a popular recreational spot, annually visited *by five hundred thousand visitors*

In 1985 *an asteroid* was named Sofiyivka after this park

# 94

# Babyn Yar

A ravine tucked away in one of Kyiv's residential neighborhoods is the site of unfathomable horror — between 100,000 and 150,000 Roma, Jews, Ukrainians, and many others were murdered here by the Nazis during the Second World War

Today, Babyn Yar is a lush park in a quiet residential area of northwestern Kyiv. In Soviet times, there were plans to build a ski facility here. But the German occupation changed these plans and forever changed the ravine. Instead, it became the site of one of the greatest massacres carried out by the Nazis during the Second World War.

At the end of September 1941, Nazi invaders occupied Kyiv, and under the threat of the death penalty, ordered all Jews in the city to gather near Babyn Yar. En mass, Kyiv's Jewish residents were ordered to undress, all their valuables were taken from them, and then, in groups, they were lined up and shot. Body after body — men, women, children — piled up in the ravine. In just two days, thirty-four thousand people were executed here. These mass executions were repeated again and again over a span of two years. The victims included Jews, Roma, prisoners of war, members of the resistance, and Soviet and Ukrainian intellectuals. In their retreat from Kyiv, the Nazis tried to hide the evidence of their crimes. But historians have managed to estimate the number of victims — somewhere between 100,000 to 150,000 people were murdered at Babyn Yar.

This horrifying massacre has been documented by Anatoly Kuznetsov in *Babi Yar: A Document in the Form of a Novel*. Kuznetsov smuggled his novel of the horrors of Babyn Yar out of Soviet Russia, and it was eventually published in the United States in 1970. The Soviets tried to hide the Jewish nature of the massacre at Babyn Yar. It was only under an independent Ukraine that memorials commemorating the fate of Jewish victims were finally erected. Kuznetsov's book ends with a chilling warning: "I have not recounted anything exceptional, but only about ordinary things that were part of a system; things that happened just yesterday, historically speaking, when people were exactly as they are today."

Twenty years later, Babyn Yar became the location of another tragedy. In 1961 the dam that crossed the ravine failed. Torrents of dirt and water broke loose on the city streets, sweeping everything away in the process — buildings, vehicles, people. This tragedy is sometimes referred to as "Kyiv's day of Pompeii" — over 1,500 people died.

*Olena Teliha Street* — located in front of Babyn Yar — is named after a well-known Ukrainian poetess who was executed in the ravine along with other nationalist writers in February of 1942

*There are numerous memorials to Babyn Yar* throughout Kyiv. At the site of the massacres you will find the 1976 monument to Soviet citizens and prisoners of war shot at Babyn Yar, and nearby, the 1991 monument to Jewish victims. There are many more throughout the city, and even internationally — in Israel, Australia, and the United States

# 95

# Kyiv Pechersk Lavra

## Lavra are large and important monasteries under direct authority of the highest church body

There are four lavras in Ukraine. The oldest and probably best known is the Dormition Kyiv Pechersk Lavra. This cave monastery was founded in 1051 in the times of Prince Yaroslav the Wise, and it became the main center for Orthodox Christianity in Kyiv Rus. Kyiv Pechersk Lavra is currently a UNESCO World Heritage Site. The most outstanding landmarks of the monastery are the Great Lavra Belltower, the Monastery Caverns, the Dormition Cathedral, the Gate Church of the Trinity, and the Necropolis of the Kyiv Pechersk Lavra. The Lavra is also home to a number of museums and the National Historical Library of Ukraine.

Another main Orthodox center in Ukraine is the Holy Dormition Pochayiv Lavra in Pochayiv, Ternopil Oblast. According to legend, this monastery was founded by Kyiv Pechersk

In the Soviet era the Sviatohirsk Lavra was liquidated and turned into a house of recreation for *the working people of Donbas.* The Dormition Cathedral became a movie theater

*The Pechersk Lavra's secret underground tunnels* have long intrigued all those who visit. They were built over a span of nine hundred years, starting in the eleventh century. You can walk through a small section today. At the moment, about 1,000 m$^2$ of the underground system has been explored

Lavra monks who escaped the Tatar invasion of 1240. The main sanctuary of this lavra holds the miraculous holy icon of the Theotokos of Pochayiv — one of the most revered icons in the Orthodox Church.

Holy Dormition Sviatohirsk Lavra in Sviatohirsk, Donetsk Oblast, is Ukraine's third spiritual sanctuary. This monastery was built on the high right bank of Siverskyi Donets (the so-called Holy Mountains). It includes a system of chalk caves, where monks still live to this day. According to some sources, this monastery has existed since the pre-Mongolian period.

The fourth Ukrainian lavra is the Greek Catholic monastery Univ Holy Dormition lavra of the Studite Rite. Among other things, this Lavra is famous for its Univ printing house, which was active between 1648 and 1770.

# NATURE

# 96

# Kalyna

A national symbol of Ukraine — you'll hear
kalyna mentioned in folksongs and depicted
in traditional embroidery and art

These merry bushes with their tas-
sels of red berries in the middle can
be found across the countryside, in every snow-covered yard — something
that is little changed from ancient

times. For Ukrainians, the kalyna, or
guelder-rose, is a symbol of life, blood
and fire. The kalyna is considered
the embodiment of femininity and,
primarily, motherhood: the bush per-

sonifies a mother, and its berries —
her children. And where the mother
resides, that is home, or motherland.

One of the most common por-
trayals of the guelder rose is as the
Tree of Light, a depiction of birds that
bring people news from the Other
World. In this way, the tree symbolizes unity between the world of the
dead and of the living.

It's no wonder that such beautiful legends, songs, poetry and fairy
tales were created around this special
representative of Ukrainian flora.
The kalyna is also considered a "wedding tree." Its berries have also come
to symbolize the courage of those
who fought for Ukraine's independence — for they are reminiscent
of drops of red blood.

# 97

# Stork

According to popular legend, storks bring newborn babies to their families

The stork is Ukrainians' most beloved bird. The bird's Ukrainian name (*leleka*) sounds a lot like the name of the ancient Slavic god of marriage and love — Lel.

In Ukrainian culture, the stork symbolizes respect for parents and the motherland; it is also a symbol for travelers and for family well-being. It's also believed that the souls of the dead come back to earth as birds.

These birds seem to share many qualities and habits with humans — traits that serve only to enhance peoples' fondness for them. In the past, people believed that storks understood human language, searched for their mate, and cared for their children just like people. In return, storks have a way of expressing their fondness for humans — by building their nests high up (in the trees or on electric poles), close to peoples' houses. It is believed that storks bring happiness to these homes.

Even today, Ukranians see storks as birds of the sun, with pure souls.

The stork is
the symbol of
the Ukrainian
Olympic team

# 98

# Nightingale

These poetic and sweetly-singing birds have a special place in Ukrainians' hearts

Ukrainians are known around the world for their singing talents — as are nightingales. A favorite of the Slavic goddesses Lada and Lelia, a symbol of youthfulness, eloquence, and great and pure talent, this bird is a very poetic representative of Ukrainian culture.

Linguists think the word *solovey* (Ukrainian for "nightingale") derives from the Old Rus *slaviy* — "one who honors God." At the same time, this bird has been considered prophetic. Nightingales are often asked to give an answer to life's philosophical questions in Ukrainian folk songs.

The nightingale is also the harbinger of spring. Nightingales start singing in Ukraine in the beginning of May when gardens are in bloom. As the old folk saying goes, a nightingale starts singing after it "drinks water from birch-tree leaves."

To hear a nightingale's song in the late summer would be an omen of impending disaster.

Numerous
*songs and poems*
are devoted to
these cherished
birds. They are
a prominent sym-
bol in Ukrainian
folk culture

# 99

# Marigolds

Happy, sunny, fragrant, and medicinal — these flowers are popular across the country

These sunny and fragrant flowers are so firmly embedded in Ukrainian everyday life, traditional medicine, folklore and rituals that it is impossible to imagine Ukraine without them.

Almost every flowerbed — whether it's next to a village house or in the middle of the city — features this plant.

Beyond their decorative purposes, marigolds are well known for their medicinal properties. They can be used to treat ailments such as headaches and toothaches.

In 2003, the music group Marigolds was created. *Black performers in vyshyvanky* singing Ukrainian folk songs deeply impressed Ukrainian viewers and listeners

These uses have evolved from traditional medicinal practices and rituals. For example, old traditions would have young boys bathe in a marigold infusion in order to encourage them to grow strong. Similarly, girls would be given their first flower garland charm at the age of three. Marigolds would feature prominently in the garland so as to ensure that the girl grew up to be pretty, with black brows and no headaches.

Marigolds can be found embroidered on shirts and rushnyky. They feature prominently in many songs, fairy tales, legends, and poems and are used in ritual to adorn icons and crosses.

# 100

# Chervona Ruta

This red plant features in folk tales and songs alike... but which plant is it?

The Chervona Ruta is a mythical plant in Ukrainian folklore, and there's a lot of speculation over which plant it actually refers to. Some think it's a flowering plant in the family Rutaceae, others place it in the genus of Rhododendron, and yet others suggest that it is white deadnettle.

According to legend, on Ivana Kupala night, the yellow ruta turns red for several minutes. Any girl who comes across this flower during the moment of its transformation is blessed with great luck. The legend might refer to two different plants. One candidate is the east-Carpathian rhododendron, which, unlike the yellow rhododendron, blooms with pink-red flowers. According to another legend, the most cherished find of Ivana Kupala night is a fern bloom, believed to be an inflamed red flower of happiness and luck. This one, however, it is meant solely for men.

In 1968, nineteen-year-old Volodymyr Ivasiuk wrote the song "Chervona Ruta." It tells a story of a girl who is searching for a magic flower to charm the one she loves (although this effort is superfluous because he loves her anyway). This song has become one of the world's most well-known Ukrainian songs.

In 1989, the music festival Chervona Ruta was founded in Ukraine.

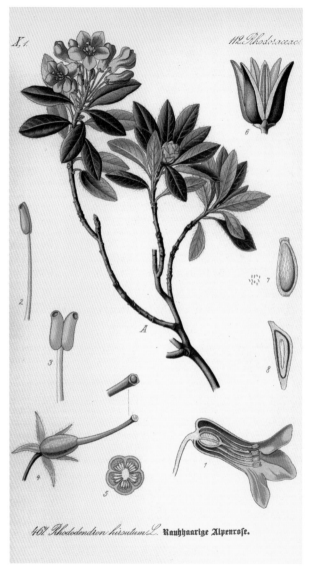

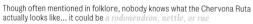

Though often mentioned in folklore, nobody knows what the Chervona Ruta actually looks like... it could be *a rodonendron, nettle, or rue*

# 101

# Dnipro River

## Flowing from Russia to the Black Sea, it is the fourth longest river in Europe

This life-giving river has a long and varied history. Dnipro means "Great River" — and great it is, flowing for over 2,200 km through three countries, providing water and electricity to several densely-populated cities along the way.

Herodotus mentioned the Dnipro long ago, in the fifth century BC. The Greeks called the river Borysthenes and believed that it had a river god-patron of the same name. Ancient Eastern Slavs called the river Slavutych (this name was given, later, to a town on the riverbank, a subway station in Kyiv, and also to numerous commercial brands). Back in the times of Kyivan Rus, the Dnipro served as a main transportation artery, connecting the Black and the Baltic Seas. Chroniclers referred to this route as "a great way from the Varangians to the Greeks." Later on, the banks of the Dnipro were home to the famous Zaporizhzhian Sich.

Up until a hydro power station was constructed in the 1960s, the Dnipro was simultaneously a source of life and a terrible threat — every spring the river flowed over its banks and flooded some districts of the city. Now, since the river's been tamed, it's a favorite place to relax and swim.

*Dnipro is a popular brand name locally* — borne by a football club, a rocket carrier, a motorcycle, a publishing house, a hotel, a subway station, and numerous other things in Kyiv and Ukraine

# 102

# Carpathian Mountains

The Carpathian mountain range stretches 1,500 km in an arc through Central and Eastern Europe

Ukraine's Carpathian region is home to several culturally and ethnically distinct groups with differing arts, crafts, and musical traditions influenced by mountain culture.

This region has spectacular, rich, dense forests. Hundred-year-old fir trees blanket the sunlight, and wanderers can gather white mushrooms and various berries on the forest floor. Violent mountain waterfalls, streams, and rivers are home to trout and other freshwater fish. The area also delights visitors with unique wooden churches, ancient castles and fortresses, and stunning mineral springs.

There is a unique *Narcissus Valley* near Khust in Zakarpattia. It's home to the largest number of white narcissus in Central Europe. Tourists from all over the world come here to witness the flowers bloom spectacularly each May

For the outdoor types, the region's national parks, reserves, and resorts offer skiing, mountain climbing, mountain biking, hiking, rafting, and caving. There are numerous health resorts with healing mineral spas. The region's distinctive mountain cultures are steeped in folklore and offer a rich culinary experience. The spectacular scenery is a must-see!

In 1996, a five-meter stele with Ukrainian national symbols — yellow-and-blue flag and tryzub — was placed on *the peak of Hoverla*, the highest mountain in the Carpathians (2061 m above sea level)

# Black Sea

What is now known as the Black Sea was once referred to as Pontos Axeinos, meaning "inhospitable sea" in Ancient Greek

In the thirteenth century, Turkish mariners called the sea *Kara Deniz*, or "black," and therefore bad.

Despite its ominous reputation, Ukraine's Black Sea today is hospitable and friendly. It has a lively sea industry, an extensive system of transportation, and is a favorite place for relaxing — as expressed by the millions of tourists who annually return to its beaches and health resorts.

The coastline of the Black Sea in Ukraine extends 1,540 km.

Most of it falls within the Crimean peninsula (which is now illegally occupied by Russia), and contains estuaries with deposits of therapeutic mud, bays, islands, peninsulas, creeks, and capes. Amazing landscapes along the southern Crimean coast, spa resorts with thermal and mineral waters, and other natural resources create a rich variety of attractions on the Black Sea.

The local climate is temperate with subtropical features that add

The Black Sea is unique due to its *hydrogen sulphide*. The sea is devoid of oxygen and therefore has no organic life below 150–200 m. There is no other such sea in the world!

to the appeal of the region's most famous resorts — Yalta, Alushta, Yevpatoria, Hurzuf, Simeyiz, and Odesa. Considering that the Black Sea coast is rich not only in recreational resources, but also in numerous historical and cultural objects, it is not surprising that this is an extremely popular tourist destination.

# 104

# Kuyalnyk Estuary

There are seven estuaries in the vicinity of Odesa. Among them, the Kuyalnyk Estuary, known for its healing mud, stands out

The first time the healing properties of the Kuyalnyk Estuary's water and mud were mentioned was in 1829, when it was called Andriyvskyi Estuary. Several years later, in 1833, Count Vorontsov ordered the construction of a hospital nearby. It was designed for taking mud, water, and sand baths. It quickly became a popular healing spot. In 1842, a new hospital building was built to replace the old one, and roads leading up to the resort were paved. These roads greatly facilitated transportation to the estuary, which is located twelve miles away from Odesa.

Previously, it was also used as a major place for salt mining. After becoming separated from the sea, Kuyalnyk's salinity increased rapidly. This estuary has been a famous place for salt mining since the Middle Ages. Wooden tools for the extraction of "white gold" have been preserved on the beaches. Today, Kuyalnyk Estuary is so shallow, that in some places, you can walk across it. Each autumn the water and the sand on the bank acquire a blood-red hue due to the withering away of the algae. This area around Kuyalnyk looks like a Martian landscape.

The Kuyalnyk spa and health resort is considered the oldest mud health resort in Ukraine. Besides the mud, which is considered the main treasure of the estuary, the was once bottled there. At one time it was supplied to the court of Catherine II

On the banks of the estuary, the remains of ancient settlements . Traces of a settlement were also found on Zhevakhova Mountain, which is adjacent to the estuary. Remains of dishes and and utensils dating back to between the sixth and second centuries BC were found

# 105

# Spiny Dogfish

This Black Sea predator is completely harmless to humans

Who would have thought that you could encounter a shark on the Black Sea coast of the Odesa Gulf? Luckily, this type of shark is harmless. The spiny dogfish, or mud shark, does not attack people, preferring to go after sprat, gobies, and anchovies. You could call it a fully fledged Odesan with that sort of diet, since that's what the people in the city tend to eat.

Spiny dogfish are also known as piked dogfish. They usually live near the coast, but they love the cold water. Therefore, encountering a spiny dogfish at an Odesa beach during peak season is practically impossible. The best time for catching a dogfish

In addition to spiny dogfish in the Black Sea, there is another type of shark which is much more rare — *the catshark*

The dimensions of this type of shark are even smaller, 60-70 cm in length, so they pose absolutely no danger to humans

This knife is also referred to as *"spiny dogfish,"* because of its form

is considered spring and autumn as the water at this time is quite cool. Additionally, a lack of bathers on the beaches allows the fish to come very close to shore.

Spiny dogfish are a kind of trophy among fishermen, and anyone who has caught one can be proud. One reason for this is that spiny dogfish are rare on the coast. The other is that they make very tasty fillets of fish. Knowing how to cook a spiny dogfish properly elevates you from an ordinary fisherman to a pro. As expected, these lucky fishermen have the pleasure of recounting the story of their catch to others.

# 106

# Sea of Azov

The shallowest sea in the world

Another body of water, the Sea of Azov, also washes Ukraine's shores. Though it's called a sea, it's not a conventional one. It looks a bit more like a lake or a reservoir (ancient Romans used to call it "the Maeotis Swamp") and has an average depth of just eight meters! There's an old joke that those who can't swim spend their vacations at the Sea of Azov.

The Sea of Azov is fed by numerous rivers and, unlike the Black Sea, has extremely low salinity and is rich in plant and fish life.

The biggest Ukrainian ports on this sea — Berdiansk and Mariupol — bring a lot of industrial pollution and pose a considerable ecological threat. Though the Sea of Azov is Europe's leader in fish resources, Ukrainian and Russian governments have concerned themselves very little with looking after it.

A system of shallow bays in the west of the sea provides an interesting attraction. Called Syvash, or the Rotten Sea, it consists of eleven lakes and bays that are very rich in salts. The deep layer of rich mud along these bays is said to have therapeutic properties — an excellent find for mud lovers.

*Peloid treatments* in the Sea of Azov are used for rheumatic disorders, osteoarthritis, gynaecological disorders, sciatica, skin diseases, trauma, and many other afflictions and ailments

Despite its size and shallowness, the sea contains the largest number of *plant and animal organisms* of any other sea in the world

# 107

# Przewalski's Horse

The Kherson Oblast in southern
Ukraine is home to a biosphere reserve:
the Askania-Nova

The reserve covers thirty-three thousand hectares with one-third of its territory holding a wildlife sanctuary. With thousands of plant and animal species, Askania-Nova is also home to one of the world's largest Przewalski horse populations.

Russian traveler and explorer Nikolay Przewalski first discovered the species in the Mongolian Steppes in 1879. Due to active horse breeding in those regions, the domestic herds forced the Przewalski horses out of their natural habitat.

Askania-Nova rests on ancient lands. The reserve is home to an open-air museum of *ancient stone statues* that are referred to as "Babi"

But this name is a misnomer, as they were erected by the Polovets tribe (Turkic) ten centuries ago and are in fact meant to represent warriors

*The Askania-Nova Reserve* (located in Kherson Oblast) started the world's first breeding program for Przewalski horses in captivity

It has helped to conserve this rare breed. Thanks to it, one of the world's largest herds of Przewalski horses presently roams the steppes

In 1899, Askania-Nova founder Friedrich Falz-Fein brought Przewalski horses to his reserve, and that's how they arrived not only in Ukraine, but also in the rest of Europe. They are a rare horse breed. Askania-Nova reserve is one of few places where they are bred.

A recently conducted experiment brought Przewalski horses to the Chornobyl "exclusion zone" in the north of the country. Not only have the horses adjusted well — but also they have successfully bred! Their population in this area now exceeds a hundred animals.

# SPORTS

# 108

# Combat Hopak

## Part martial art, part dance

Zaporizhian kozaks transformed the hopak dance into a martial art. According to some researchers, it was a kind of kozak wushu. Complex techniques of combat fighting could be practiced in hopak, along with other dances, challenging a fighter's lung capacity and endurance in the process. Thus, "with a song and a dance" and holding a heavy saber in each hand at the same time, kozaks acquired their exceptional fighting mastery.

In the 1980s, a native of Lviv named Volodymyr Pylat set out to revive this martial art based on many elements that were preserved in the folk dances and traditions of our forefathers' fighting techniques. In 1987, the School of Combat Hopak was founded. Today this martial art has grown in popularity, sparking a youth movement. Schools dedicated to this combat style have popped up across Ukraine and in North America.

In 2001, *the Ukrainian Combat Hopak team* took third place at the IV World Martial Arts Festival in Southern Korea — astonishing the international martial arts scene and gaining prestige for the sport

In 2002, *a school of Ukrainian women's martial arts* Asharda was founded

# 109

# Ivan Piddubnyi

When this Ukrainian wrestler and six-time world champion was asked, "Who is the love of your life ?" he answered, "Ukraine, of course, who else?"

Descended from an old kozak family, Piddubnyi could easily wrestle a cow down to the ground by the horns. He worked as a loader in Crimean ports for a long time and later performed as a strongman in circuses.

At the beginning of the twentieth century, Ivan Piddubnyi committed himself to professional wrestling with great success, and he managed to conquer first Europe and then the entire world with his technique

and strength. It took him only four years (from 1905 to 1909) to become the world champion six times over. For a quarter of a century he remained undefeated. Piddubnyi repeatedly attributed his success not just to his brawn, but to his brains too —he was a quick-thinking athlete.

Piddubnyi's career as a professional wrestler was successful, but short. He would later work in the circus into old age. He spent the last

When Piddubnyi was issued a passport which stated that he is Russian, *he corrected his nationality to Ukrainian*

During the German (Nazi) occupation, Piddubnyi refused to leave the Soviet Union to train *German wrestlers*

years of his life in poverty, selling his trophies to buy food.

Our contemporaries have forgotten Piddubnyi's name, though for a long time this prominent sportsman personified the harmony of body and spirit for Ukrainians. He was a true Ukrainian patriot, even during the turbulent Soviet years.

# 110

# FC Dynamo

## The internationally renowned Dynamo is Ukraine's most sucessful and popular football club

It is the most titled club, not only in Ukraine, but in the entire former Soviet Union. The club's achievements include dozens of Cups and Super Cups in national and USSR championships, a UEFA Super Cup and two Cup Winners' Cups.

FC Dynamo Kyiv was founded in 1927 and was then known for its "Chekist" affiliations. "Chekists" were members of the Soviet Union's first state security organisation. Despite professionalization over the years, the club maintained connections with the state

As part of the Soviet Union until its collapse in December 1991, the club has also won *13 USSR Championships, 9 USSR Cups, and 3 USSR Super Cups,* making Dynamo the most successful club in the history of the Soviet Top League

security apparatus until the collapse of the USSR.

In the 1990s, Kyiv Dynamo became privately owned by Hryhoriy Surkis. Some of the club's most notable players include Serhiy Rebrov, Andriy Shevchenko, Leonid Buriak, and Oleh Blokhin, who played 586 matches and scored 270 goals for Dynamo. No mention of Dynamo would be complete without honoring its most prominent coach — Valeriy Lobanovskyi (1939–2002). He was elected head coach thrice and led the team to win the Cup Winners' Cup twice. Dynamo's main rival clubs are FC Arsenal Kyiv (Kyiv derby) and Shakhtar (Donetsk).

# 111

# Valeriy Lobanovskyi

Valeriy Lobanovskyi (1939–2002) began his professional football career with FC Dynamo Kyiv in 1957

Though he only played for the club for five years, his name is forever associated with it. At the age of twenty-nine, Lobanovskyi left his football career to take the position of coach for Dnipropetrovsk FC Dnipro. Within five years he returned to Dynamo in this role. Shortly after becoming coach he introduced his signature tactical approach to training and led the team to become the number one football team in the USSR and winners of the UEFA Winners Cup and Super Cup.

Valeriy Lobanovskyi was three times elected head coach of the USSR football team and three times became Dynamo head coach. He dedicated many years to the club. Under Lobanovskyi's coaching, Dynamo won the Cup Winners' Cup twice, the championship of the USSR eight times and the Cup of the USSR six times!

After a period of absence, Valeriy Lobanovskyi returned to Dynamo in 1997 to lead his native club to the UEFA Champions League semifinals, giving him a new chance to enter the "high society" of European football.

After Valeriy Lobanovskyi's death in May 2002, Dynamo — having lost its mentor — failed to win the Championship of Ukraine for the very first time.

Following his death, Lobanovskyi was awarded the title *Hero of Ukraine*, the nation's highest honor. Dynamo Kyiv's Stadium was renamed the Lobanovskyi Stadium in his honor

# 112

# Oleh Blokhin

## Renowned as a standout striker, Blokhin led Ukraine to the World Cup quarterfinals in 2006

Oleh Blokhin started his career in FC Dynamo Kyiv, where he played from 1969 to 1987 and earned the title of USSR Top Score. In 1975 he was awarded the world's most prestigious football trophy: the Golden Ball Award. Blokhin also holds the title of Best Scorer in the History of the USSR Championships, the best scorer of the USSR team of all times (42 goals) as well as numerous other titles, achievements and awards.

Following an outstanding football career, Oleh Blokhin turned his skills to coaching in 1990 and spent several years coaching Greek football clubs. In 2003, Blokhin became the head coach of the Ukrainian national team. He demonstrated his talents at the World Cup in 2006. After a two-year break in coaching the national team, Blokhin returned to the head coach position in April 2011.

In 1975 he was named *European Footballer of the Year*, winning the Ballon d'Or, becoming the first Ukrainian player to achieve such a feat

Today, despite the numerous records and awards Blokhin gained in Soviet football, in the minds of Ukrainians he remains the only man to have coached Ukraine at major football finals. In 2011 he was named a Legend of Ukrainian Football together with Igor Belanov and Vitali Starukhin at the Victory of Football Awards.

# 113

# Andriy Shevchenko

Affectionately called "Sheva," this great sportsman is universally adored

Born in 1976, Shevchenko is an internationally famous football player — a prolifically talented top scorer. Shevchenko embodies the "Ukrainian dream" — he rose through sheer talent from humble and difficult beginnings. At a young age, his family had to flee their home due to the radiation effects of the Chornobyl disaster.

Shevchenko is a fan favorite. Thousands of young football enthusiasts sport Shevchenko's number 7 shirt in emulation of their mentor. Whether that shirt is in black-and-red A.C. Milan stripe, the blue-and-yellow colors of Ukraine's na-tional team, or in the white-and-blue Dynamo stripe, it is a symbol of great success!

Shevchenko's talents have been widely recognized with awards for best player and best scorer. He was twice awarded the Bronze Ball and once the Golden Ball in 2004. The list goes on.

In 2011, Shevchenko won a silver medal in a Ukrainian golf championship. This gives us hope that, upon finishing his career in football, he will continue to bring Ukraine glory as an out-standing golfer atop his many other accomplishments!

In his incredibly successful international career, the striker led Ukraine as captain to the quarterfinals in their first ever *FIFA World Cup* appearance in 2006

# 114

# FC Shakhtar Donetsk

## This Donetsk football club has few rivals in popularity

Founded in 1936, this club's football prowess had a slow start. It wasn't until the 1960s that Shakhtar gained renown at the USSR championships, but after that the club, over the Soviet period the club won four USSR Cups (1961, 1962, 1980, and 1983) and one Super Cup (1984).

In the mid-1990s, Rinat Akhmetov (Ukraine's richest businessman) became president of the club. After this, things quickly started to look up for Shakhtar. Considerable financ-

Since 1961 the official colors of Shakhtar club have been *black and orange*

ing and players' transfers made Shakhtar a leader at the Ukrainian championship and turned the club into a worthy rival for European teams. In 2004, fortune favored them again when experienced coach Mircea Lucescu became Shakhtar's main mentor. Since his arrival, Shakhtar has become the national champion five times and the three-time winner of the Ukrainian Super Cup.

The club's home arena is the five-star stadium Donbas Arena — considered the best stadium in Ukraine! Sadly, the conflict in the east has badly damaged the stadium and it is presently being used as a distribution center for refugees. Since 2014, FC Shakhtar Donetsk has played in exile.

*Shakhtar became the first club in independent Ukraine to win the UEFA Cup in 2009*, the last year before the competition was revamped as the Europa League

# 115

# Serhiy Bubka

Champion of Champions. That's what French newspaper L'Equipe called Serhiy Bubka in 1997, declaring him the best sportsman in the world

World Champion, European Champion, USSR Champion, Olympic Champion — Serhiy Bubka (born in 1963) was among the top ten sportsmen in the USSR and is listed in the Guinness World Records for having the greatest number of achievements in athletics.

Bubka broke thirty-five world records in all. The fifth one — when Bubka cleared 6.0 meters — is of particular significance. Taking place in Paris, this jump was called "the jump of the future" because it started a new era in pole vaulting. Serhiy Bubka's last record of 6.15 meters remained undefeated for over twenty years.

It is thanks to this Ukrainian sportsman that there is an increased interest in pole vaulting.

Today Serhiy Bubka heads the National Olympic Committee of Ukraine. He holds the title of Hero of Ukraine. A monument in honor of this outstanding athlete can be found in Donetsk.

Serhiy Bubka
holds two
world records:
the outdoor
world record of
*6.14 meters*, set
on July 31, 1994, in
Sestriere, Italy,
and the indoor
world record of
6.15 meters, set on
February 21, 1995, in
Donetsk, Ukraine

# 116

# Vitali and Volodymyr Klitschko

Heavyweight boxing champions

These brothers — Vitali (born in 1971) and Volodymyr (born in 1976) — have taken the boxing world by storm. After Volodymyr's victory at the Olympics in Atlanta (1996), the brothers started their professional careers under the supervision of German trainer Fritz Zdunek. From their first victories by knockout, they proved to be very dangerous opponents.

Starting in 1998, these prominent boxers have been determinedly taking the belts of the most authoritative boxing associa-

Vitali Klitschko is presently *the mayor of Kyiv* and was a prominent political figure during Ukraine's Euromaidan Revolution. He holds a PhD in sports science

Volodymyr Klitschko, is *the WBA (Super), IBF, WBO, IBO and The Ring World Heavyweight Champion*

tions from the world's best boxers. On June 2, 2011, after Volodymyr Klitschko's victory over the British David Haye, the brothers — having united their accomplishments — became owners of champion belts in the heavyweight category of the four most prestigious international boxing organizations.

Vitali and Volodymyr are not just exceptional sportsmen — but they also have brains! Both brothers are involved in politics and philanthropy and are avid chess players. Vitali has put his boxing career aside and is currently the mayor of Kyiv.

# 117

# Gymnastics

## Ukraine is one of the world's leaders for gymnastics countries

From the Soviet era to now, Ukrainian athletes have excelled in artistic and rhythmic gymnastics. Native of Kherson Larysa Latynina, a native of Kherson, has an outstanding sports career that deserves a special mention. She is a nine-time Olympic champion in artistic gymnastics.

The most renowned gymnast of independent Ukraine is Lilia Podkopayeva (born in 1978). She was a champion of the Atlanta Olympic Games. Sadly, Lilia's burgeoning career was cut short at the early age of nineteen due to serious leg trauma. She is currently coaching and designing clothing for gymnastics and is the organizer of the Golden Lily tournament.

The godmother of the Ukrainian school of rhythmic gymnastics is Iryna Deriuhina (born in 1958), the only Soviet gymnast who was the twice World Champion (1977 and 1979). Upon finishing her sporting career, Deriuhina was appointed coach of the National Ukrainian team together with her mother, Albina Deriuhina. The Deriuhinas managed to bring up an entire generation of outstanding rhythmic gymnasts and Olympic champions, among them Oleksandra Tymoshenko, Kateryna Serebrianska, and Hanna Bezsonova. The Deriuhina Cup, an international competition, is held annually in Kyiv.

*Hanna Rizatdinova* is a Ukrainian individual rhythmic gymnast, she is the 2016 Olympic bronze medalist, a two-time World medalist (silver in 2013, bronze in 2014), and a two-time (2014, 2016) European bronze medalist

*Lilia Pod-kopayeva's* signature move — double-front somersault with half-twist — has yet to be repeated by anyone

# 118

# Paralympians

Ukraine has been amongst the top medal winners in both recent summer and winter Paralympic Games

Ukraine made its Paralympic Games début at the 1996 Summer Paralympics in Atlanta, with thirty athletes competing in archery, track and field, powerlifting, swimming, and volleyball. Since then, Ukraine has competed at every of the Summer and Winter Games since then and has done so with remarkable success. Ukrainian athletes have won a total of 257 Paralympic medals.

One of the most successful Ukrainian paralympians is swimmer Maskym Veraksa. Veraksa is wide-ly regarded as the world's fastest Paralympic swimmer as the world record holder of 22.99 seconds in the men's 50 m freestyle. That record has stood since 2009 and is one of the oldest in Paralympic swimming.

At the latest Games in Rio de Janeiro, Ukraine's Paralympics team finished the competition winning 117 medals, of which 41 were gold medals, 37 silver, and 39 bronze. This made Ukraine third in the medal table. One of the winners was Oksana Zubkovska, who secured her third straight

Valeriy Sushkevych, a former disability swimmer turned politician and member of Parliament, has been credited with *"kick-starting the Paralympic movement in the country."* He helped establish *a national Paralympic center in 2002* and ensured that Ukrainian Paralympians were granted a separate budget

Paralympic gold medal in the long jump with an effort of 6.11 meters.

Petro Poroshenko, the president of Ukraine, has described the performance of the Ukrainian Paralympians as "incredible," adding that the athletes prove "that the impossible is possible."

# TECHNOLOGY

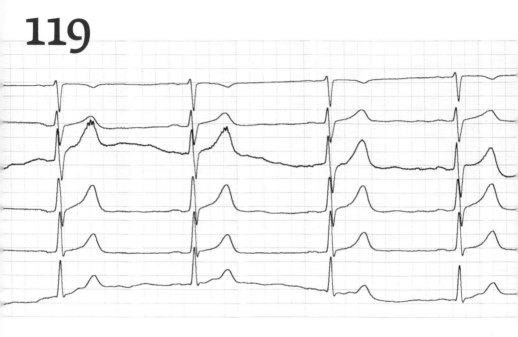

# 119

# Mykola Amosov

World-renowned heart surgeon, founder of bio-cybernetics in Ukraine, and a prolific writer — Amosov's contributions are manifold

Occasionally, solitary geniuses emerge in culture and science, whose ideas and innovations spread throughout the globe. Mykola Amosov is one such individual.

Amosov was born to Russian peasants, fought in the Second World War, and ended up mov-ing to Kyiv to practice medicine in the mid-1960s. With interests bridging medicine and technolo-gy, he established new techniques in his field, with particular con-tributions in the areas of cardi-ac surgery and biocybernetics. Amosov performed more than six

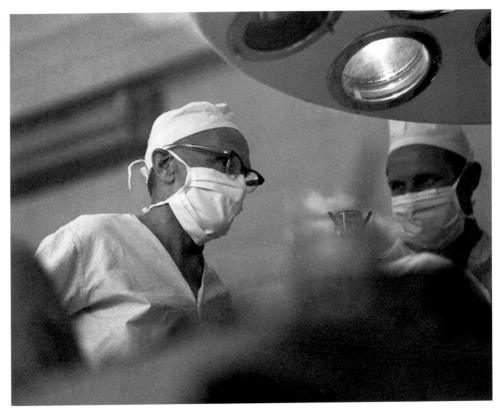

Amosov was vocal about how hard it was to deal with patient deaths. This was the subject of his first short novel *Thoughts and the Heart* (1967)

In 2003 the Institute of Cardiovascular Surgery of Ukraine was *named after Amosov*

thousand heart surgeries, many of them with extracorporeal blood circulation. He was the first person in the USSR to create a mitral valve prosthesis.

Beyond medicine, Amosov dedicated a lot of attention to psychology and sociology. The range of his research was impressive: from artificial intelligence to the global problems of mankind and matters of the heart. He authored hundreds of publications, and his contributions to the world of science, technology, and medicine are prolific.

# 120

# Donbas

## Ukraine's industrial heartland which gets its name from its location in the Donets River Basin

It is considered the industrial center of Ukraine and, as natives of Donbas claim, the harshest region in Europe.

The city of Donetsk stands at the center of Donbas. It was built up round a steel plant built by foreign investors in 1869. The majority of cities in this region were established in a similar way, popping up around factories, plants, and mines.

Donbas has merciless heat in summer and relentless winter frosts. The landscape is dotted by endless chains of slag heaps, mines, pipes, and hundreds of plants and factories surrounded by bare steppe.

In 2014 Donbas has been occupied by pro-Russian rebels and Russian troops, sparking a massive humanitarian crisis. With many inhabitants of the region forced to flee, these hard-working people are still waiting for peace so they can return to their homes.

Massive
abandoned
slag heaps dot
*the Donbas
landscape*

*Top: Now You Can Have a Smoke. Oleksiy Stakhanov with Young Miners, 1949*

# 121

# Coal

## When industrial coal mining in Ukraine started to take off, being a miner became one of the most prestigious working-class occupations

The industry peaked in the mid-1970s when more than two hundred million tons of coal per year was mined. Since these peak years, there have been successive mine closures due to bankruptcy. For towns and cities in the eastern region of the Donbas, these closures have led to a massive loss in employment and economic stagnation.

The Donbas is mostly a steppe zone. In the past seventy years, the landscape of Donetsk and Luhansk Oblasts has been changed by slag heaps, which are large mountain-like artificial mounds of coal mining waste.

The mining industry once brought opportunity for employment to the region, but it came at a cost. These enormous slag heaps stand like monuments to the many mining catastrophes that have happened here. This scarred landscape offers a constant reminder that the impacts of mining persist long after the industry stops here, with lives lost, polluted environments, and negative impacts on human health.

The mining industry has left its mark on the eastern regions, not only environmentally, but socially, politically, and linguistically.

More than 90 percent of Ukraine's coal production comes from *the Donetsk Basin*. Ukrainian coal mines are among the most dangerous in the world, and accidents are common. Ukraine is also plagued by extremely dangerous illegal mines

# 122

# An-225 Mriya

## Mriya is the largest and heaviest transport aircraft in the world

The An-225 can fly at speeds of up to 850 km/h and can cover distances of close to 15,000 kilometers. It's capable of lifting more than 250 tons of cargo into the air — a re-

cord-setting capacity. This giant was created at the Antonov Design Bureau in Kyiv in 1988 for the purposes of space exploration. Upon the collapse of the USSR, most

*The Antonov An-225 carrying the Buran space shuttle*

of the space programs in Ukraine were cancelled. Today Mriya is used as an aircraft for non-standard and ultra-heavy cargo: locomotives, 150–200-ton generators, humanitarian missions of especially great amounts, etc. An-225 is currently the main transport engine in the Antonov Airlines aircraft park. It is frequently requested by other countries to transport extra-large cargo.

Presently Mriya is the only one of its kind in existence. Even though another aircraft of this size is being constructed and is about 70 percent finished, about $120 million is required to complete its construction.

# 123

# Zaporozhets

One of Soviet Ukraine's most popular cars, which still inspires ironic smiles for its longevity, tenacity and nostalgia

The prototype for the Zaporozhets was the famous Fiat-600, the Seicento, and was no less significant for Soviet citizens than the European Beetle is for Europeans. Taking after the traditions of European automobiles of the time, the Zaporozhets featured rear-wheel

The name Zaporozhets means kozak of *the Zaporizhian Sich*. It can also refer to a man from Zaporizhzhya Oblast

drive and — because of its specific body form — it was given the nickname "the Hunchback." It is a car with a long legacy, having been manufactured since 1960. The Zaporizhian Automobile Factory continued to produce a slightly altered Zaporozhets with no major modernizations up until 1994. This long legacy has given birth to numerous anecdotes. With production starting in the 1970s, this automobile was cheap, but it was not technologically up to date. As such, it became a symbol of Soviet stagnation — the period of economic difficulty and lack of reform.

Nowadays Zaporozhets cars are frequently used as art objects or for spare parts. They can be found painted in wild colors and turned into convertibles, big foots, etc.

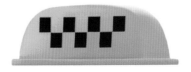

# 124

# Lanos

## Designed by the Korean company Daewoo and produced in Ukraine

The Zaporizhia Automobile Building Plant has been one of the biggest producers of Daewoo Lanos cars since 2003. At first, the components were shipped from Korea, Romania, and Poland. But starting in 2008 the car became entirely Ukrainian: bodywork and engine production included.

Thanks to comparatively low prices, the accessibility of auto parts, and its simple and relatively reliable construction, the Lanos has truly become a people's car. It's the working pony of Ukrainian driving, with more than a quarter of today's Ukrainian taxis being Lanos.

While the Lanos is often scorned by snobs because of its classification as a cheap C-class car, it's better than many other domestic and other post-Soviet countries' vehicles in terms of safety, value for money, and public recognition.

Lanos is the unofficial vehicle of Ukrainian *taxi drivers*

People commonly modify these cars — adding skirts, front and rear bumpers, spoilers, splitters, air vents, and light weight wheels. ***Illegal racing*** on pimped-out Lanoses is also popular

# 125

# An-124 Ruslan

## The largest series cargo aircraft in the world

There are fifty-six units of these "sky titans." Forty of them are operated by Ukrainian, Russian Libyan, and Arab Emirate airlines. The Ruslan was designed and created by Antonov Design Bureau in Kyiv during the Cold War. Back then its many features surpassed even the most powerful transport aircraft in the US — the C-5 Galaxy — and it became a real threat to the West. The Ruslan aircraft gave Soviet authorities considerable strategic mobility.

Nowadays Ruslan is somewhat modernized and serves as a military transport airplane. It accounts for hundreds of heavy and extraordinary cargo planes. For example, in 1992 Ruslan transported fifty-two tons of gold from UAE to Switzerland.

The aircraft is able to "kneel" to allow for easier front loading. Up to **150 tons** of cargo can be carried in a military An-124

In 1993, it took Michael Jackson three such planes to transfer more than three hundred tons of his concert equipment to Moscow. In the autumn of 2011, Ruslan also transported special cargo to Japan: eighty-six-ton pumps for the liquidation of the nuclear disaster at Fukushima 1.

# 126

# Yevhen Paton

## Paton's innovative bridge designs have left an indelible mark on Kyiv

Paton was one of the most important scientific minds of the industrial epoch in Ukraine. He pioneered innovations in welding and joining for a variety of purposes, but in Kyiv he is most well known for his bridges.

Upon finishing his studies in Dresden and St. Petersburg, the French-born Paton took up research and teaching. The Paton Bridge over the Dnipro is among Paton's most prominent work. It was built in 1953 and was the world's first all-welded bridge. The bridge stretches more than one and a half kilometers in length. Unfortunately, Yevhen Paton never witnessed its completion — he died three months before the opening of his creation.

Kyiv residents have a special fondness for another of Paton's bridges — the "Lovers' Bridge" across a ravine in Maryinskyi Park. Beyond bridges, Paton's legacy includes 350 scientific papers.

Built in 1941-53, this was *the world's first all-welded bridge* and is also the longest bridge in Kyiv, with a length of 1,543 meters

# 127

# Rapeseed

**Ukraine has always been an agricultural country, and this is one of its major crops**

Ukraine's vast territory and fertile black soils (covering 44 percent of the territory) make for ideal growing conditions. It's no wonder Ukraine is often referred to as the "breadbasket of Europe."

Rapeseed is a very common crop. With its bright yellow flower and oil-rich seed, it is the third largest source of vegetable oil in the world. Rapeseed cultivation fell out of favor during the Soviet era and was replaced with sunflower crops. But its cultivation is making a comeback thanks in part to a growing demand for biofuel. In 2007 Ukraine introduced tax benefits for biofuel producers, which has spurred this industry. Ukraine is one of the world's largest exporters of rapeseed.

Some say that rapeseed presents *an ecological danger* to Ukraine. Rapeseed cultivation can leach nutrients from Ukraine's rich black soil, and its extensive cultivation can lead to poor monoculture practices

133 bis
B . Na.

133
*Brassica*
*sativa*
a . B. Napus

# 128

# STALKER

## An endlessly pliable allegory about human consciousness

The 1979 cult film *Stalker* by Russian director Andrei Tarkovsky was based on a script by Arkadyi and Boris Strugatsky. Did they know that they would give rise to a movement of stalker mania?

In 2007, the Ukrainian company GSC Game World issued the legendary computer game S.T.A.L.K.E.R.: Shadow of Chernobyl that won over the hearts of millions of gaming fans. The game sold more than two million official copies in its first year alone and more than ten million pirated ones! These figures don't even account for all of the illegally downloaded versions.

The Stalker franchise sold *over four million copies*

This game became especially popular in the countries of the former Soviet Union due to the gritty realism of its portrayal of industrial regions and the action's location — the Chornobyl zone. The gigantic S.T.A.L.K.E.R. universe has become a parallel reality for many fans of this computer game. Beyond the three games of the series (Shadow of Chernobyl, Clear Sky and Call of Pripyat), there are numerous books set in the game's world. Amateurs shoot short films, and fans organize role games and illegal raids within the Chornobyl exclusion zone.

Fans of the game and the movie can experience the real thing: some Ukrainian companies offer visits to *the exclusion zone of Prypiat* and Chornobyl. These questionable tours cost around $50

# 129

# Ihor Sikorskyi

The future designer of famous amphibious helicopters built his first aircrafts in the backyard of a local Kyiv house

Ihor Sikorskiy was an innovator. He was born in 1889 into the family of a Kyiv University professor. From early childhood, he was fond of science and adored the drawings of Leonardo da Vinci. Even as he studied at Kyiv Polytechnical Institute, Ihor started crafting models of helicopters in the field of his father's house at Yaroslaviv Val Street. By 1911, he had set the world flight speed record, piloting an aircraft of his own design.

*Ihor Sikorskiy's* famous hat can be found at his company's museum. Test pilots have adopted the ritual of touching the hat before a test flight

*The Sikorsky H-34 is a piston-engined military helicopter used by the US Army*

Soon, Sikorskiy designed the world's first multi-engine aircraft, the Russian Champion (the "Grand") and the legendary bomber, the Ilya Muromets, becoming becoming a sort of celebrity in the Russian Empire. With the Revolution of 1917, the designer decided to emigrate. He moved to the United States and started his own company, the Sikorsky Aircraft Corporation, which remains a leading aircraft design company to this day.

Ihor Sikorskiy designed several airplanes and helicopters, yet he always considered his greatest achievement to be the invention of an amphibious helicopter, which was able to land on water. This invention has saved the lives of thousands of people caught in natural disasters.

In the Sikorsky Aircraft's first years, the company was saved from bankruptcy by a well-known composer, **Sergei Rachmaninov**. He lent Ihor *$5,000,* a considerable amount of money at that time

# 130

# Port of Odesa

## Ukraine's largest port and major transportation hub

The Odesa Port was established on the same day as the founding of the city itself, on the September 2, 1794. It was that day that the first posts were driven into the Large and Small piers. The head of the port was Odesa's first mayor José de Ribas. The *porto franco* (free port) status, assigned in 1819, had a significant impact on its development. The Odesa harbor quickly became the second largest in terms of cargo turnover in the Russian Empire after St. Petersburg. At the end of the nineteenth century, the port's cargo turnover grew to double that of St. Petersburg's.

The development of the port contributed to the emergence of the Potemkin Steps, which connect the city of Odesa to its harbor below and are considered an entrance

TECHNOLOGY AWESOME UKRAINE

The Odesa port was the base of the Black Sea Shipping Company. *It was founded in 1863* and was the oldest on the Black Sea. In addition, the Black Sea Shipping Company was *the largest in Europe in terms of number of vessels.* After the collapse of the USSR, *the company went bankrupt and all the ships were sold*

There is also an oil and gas terminal at the Port of Odesa. The terminal is the biggest one in Ukraine: it has six berths with a total storage capacity of *671,000 m³*

to the city from the port. The red brick warehouses in the Karantynna port became its symbol, along with the Vorontsov Lighthouse.

During the Crimean War, the port was bombed by a Franco-British squadron. In commemoration of this, a rifle from the *Tiger* frigate warship, which sank near the harbor, was installed near City Hall. The port also played a key role during World War II, as it was a strategic site from which people could evacuate the city.

When Ukraine became independent, the port of Odesa became the largest cargo handling and passenger traffic port in the country. Each year, the largest passenger liners in the world enter the Odesa marina.

# 131

# Sunflower

Sunflowers, sonyashnyky, are Ukraine's most profitable agrarian product

They are Ukraine's national flower, and in folk imagery represent the warmth and power of the sun. Beyond that, Ukraine is one of the world's largest producers and exporters of sunflower seeds and sunflower oil.

Sunflowers require a certain number of sunny days a year, in order to have an enzymatic process of oil formation in the seeds. Due to Ukraine's unique natural climatic conditions

Sunflower seed was *the most profitable agrarian product of Ukraine* in 2015

sunflowers grow in almost all territories of Ukraine, but mostly in the south of the country. You will see huge sunflower fields on the road to Odesa, for example.

Ukrainians are fond of everything that comes from the sunflower plant: oil for cooking, and everyone likes chewing on sunflower seeds while having a chat with their neighbors in a courtyard.

Ukrainian experts grew *the tallest sunflower* in 2011, its height was 4m 17cm

# 132

# IT Industry

Ukraine's IT industry is famous all the world over, with Ukrainians becoming part of the global digital civilisation

Four generations of engineers and specialists have aided the development of Ukraine's IT sector from the middle of the twentieth century until the present day. The first generation of specialists created Europe's first digital computer, Sergey Lebedev's MESM (*mala elektronna rahuvalna mashyna*). The second, under Victor Glushkov's direction, created a prototype of the Internet in 1964, whilst the Americans had barely created their model of the ARPANET connection. The third generation built large-scale data processing and analysis centers across cities in Ukraine. The fourth generation has finally managed to export their technology after Ukraine's independence.

Ukraine's IT sector employs nearly 150,000 people, with growth rates rising each year. Factoring in related industries, that's about **450,000 people involved with IT in Ukraine!** IT services make up about 4 percent of Ukraine's GDP, which makes up about $4.5 million

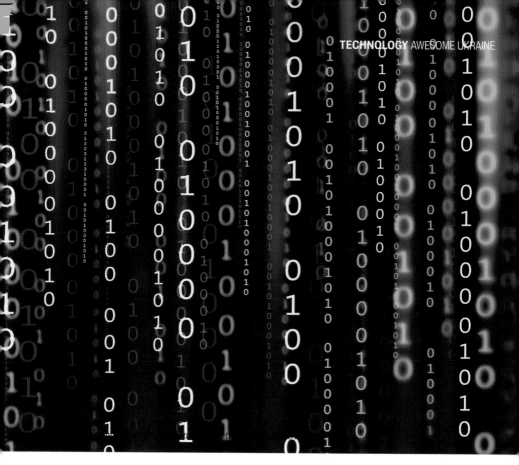

Nowadays IT is mostly based on outsourcing to Ukraine. This has led to the creation of powerful economic IT clusters, but Ukraine also has its own domestic companies, the number of which is still growing. They have already made a sizeable contribution to developments in global digital technology — today, Ukrainian startups such as PetCube, Grammarly, and Depositphotos are known all over the world.

With the war in Eastern Ukraine, unfortunately cyber warfare had a chance to develop: Ukraine became a battleground for a cyber war after a series of cyberattacks. Still, this meant that Ukraine gained the potential to become a leading center for research in and the development of cybersecurity.

In the 1960s cyber researchers and engineers decided to jokingly create their own *virtual country: Cybertonia*. They even created their own newspaper, passports, and a government structure. Cybertonia's subculture brought together many experts and developed new technologies

**133**

134

135

# AWESOME Series

More from Awesome Series: Awesome Odesa, Awesome Kyiv,
Awesome Kharkiv, Awesome Lviv. There you will find all that we love
about these Ukrainian cities — from national dishes to historical facts,
symbols, mythology, popular culture and much more.
Awesome Digital coming soon!

Order now on our website! **osnovypublishing.com**